Christmas

in WALES

Also edited by Dewi Roberts

A Clwyd Anthology
Birdsong
Childhood

Christmas
in WALES

An anthology edited by Dewi Roberts

SEREN

Seren is the book imprint of
Poetry Wales Press Ltd
Nolton Street, Bridgend, Wales
www.serenbooks.com

Editorial and Introduction © Dewi Roberts, 1997
For individual contributions see Acknowledgements

First published 1997. Reprinted 1998, 2004, 2005, 2006, 2007, 2010

ISBN 1-85411-186-8

The publisher works with the financial assistance
of the Welsh Books Council.

Cover photograph: Dave Newbould
                www.davenewbould.co.uk

Printed in Plantin by Bell & Bain, Glasgow

Mixed Sources
Product group from well-managed
forests and other controlled sources
www.fsc.org   Cert no. TT-COC-002769
© 1996 Forest Stewardship Council

Contents

9   *Introduction*

Advent to Christmas Eve

15   Hilary Llewellyn-Williams — Holly
16   Vernon Watkins — Midwinter
16   Gillian Clarke — Midwinter
17   Michael Gareth Llewelyn — An Old World Custom
19   Vernon Watkins — *from* The Ballad of the Mari Llwyd
21   Ruth Bidgood — First Snow
22   Janet Dubé — Advent Poem for Jo
23   R.S. Thomas — The Qualities of Christmas
25   Peter Finch — Some Christmas Haiku
26   Gwyn Thomas — Scrooge, A Defence
28   Ruth Bidgood — Magpies at Christmas
29   Douglas Phillips — Christmas at Pentrepoeth School,
                         Carmarthen
30   Glyn Jones —Pugh, the Festive Policeman
32   Siân James — Mother Christmas
33   R.S. Thomas — Carol
33   Bruce Chatwin — The Nativity Play
36   Tony Curtis — The Infants' Christmas Concert
37   Herbert Williams — Billy Scrooge and the Santagram
39   Idris Davies — A Star In The East
40   Eiluned Lewis — A Sad Dark Tune
42   Peter Finch — More Christmas Haiku
43   Kate Roberts — The Battle of Christmas
44   Gwyn Thomas — Lifting the Curse of Shabbiness
45   Kate Roberts — Pricking the Bubble
48   Gwyn Thomas — Ogley the Abstainer
51   Gillian Clarke — Snow
51   Emlyn Williams — Hard Times
52   Leslie Norris — Maldwyn
54   Paul Henry — Inside the MIND Shop
55   Richard Burton — Radicalism on Christmas Eve
57   Edith Courtney — A Visit to Kilvey Hill
59   Dewi Roberts — The Invitation
62   Meic Stephens — Dymuniad y Tymor
63   Ronnie Knox Mawer — Gifts from the Chemist's Shop

64 Kate Roberts — Buying the Cards
65 A.J. Cronin — Grateful Patients
65 Irene Thomas — Christmas Goose
67 Leslie Norris — Great, Invisible Birds
70 Idris Davies — Christmas Eve 1946
71 Ruth Bidgood — Solstice
72 Gladys Mary Coles —Touching Balloons, Llandudno
73 Selyf Roberts — A Wartime Exile
75 Richard Hughes — Bedtime Anticipation
76 Joseph P. Clancy — A Cywydd for Christmas

Christmas Day

79 Rowland Watkyns — Upon Christ's Nativity or Christmas
79 Francis Kilvert — An Icy Bath
80 Eiluned Lewis — A Victorian Festive Service
81 Catherine Fisher — Nativity
82 R.S. Thomas — Christmas
82 Thomas Love Peacock — A Festive Gathering at
                                                 Headlong Hall
84 Nigel Wells — Y Plygaint
86 Francis Kilvert — A Christmas Day Funeral
87 Huw Jones — Christmas Card
88 Dylan Thomas — That Bright White Snowball of Christmas
90 Harri Webb — Christmas Cheer
92 Mike Jenkins — Turkeys Aren't Pets
93 Robert Minhinnick — A Christmas Story
94 Gwyn Thomas — Gifts
95 Mike Jenkins — The Essence of Presents
96 Alun Llewelyn-Williams — Star of Bethlehem
97 Dylan Thomas — A Festive Letter to Pamela Hansford
                                                 Johnson
99 John Wain — Christmas in Gwynedd
100 Phil Carradice — Christmas Day at Pembroke
101 Rhydwen Williams — Christmas in the Valley
104 Iorwerth Peate — The Craftsman's Carol
105 Alun Lewis — A Letter from India
107 Idris Davies — The Christmas Tree
107 T.H. Parry-Williams — A Christmas Carol
108 Jean Earle — Holy and Practical Matters
109 R.S. Thomas — Hill Christmas

110   Saunders Lewis — Carol
110   D.J. Williams — A Pagan Custom
112   Angharad Tomos — A Domestic Scene
114   Bobi Jones — Sickness at Christmas
114   E. Tegla Davies — Reflections on Mortality
116   Ifor Thomas — Christmas Drink
116   Alun Lewis — Christmas Holiday
117   Mary Davies Parnell — A Rhondda Christmas
119   John Idris Jones — Berwyn Christmas
122   Saunders Lewis — Under the Mistletoe
124   Denis F. Ratcliffe — A Difficult Christmas
126   Margiad Evans — Christmases
126   A.J. Cronin — Tom Evans' Pride
128   Tom Macdonald — The Christmas Eisteddfod
131   Mary Davies Parnell — Sampling the Wine
132   Tony Curtis — Christmas Poem at Tenby Harbour
133   Ray Milland — The Day of Delights
135   Stuart Nolan — An Adult's Christmas in Wales

Boxing Day to Epiphany

141   Chris Bendon — Slow
143   Emlyn Williams — A Boxing Day Treat
144   Dannie Abse — Pantomime Diseases
145   Roland Mathias — After Christmas
145   James Williams — Killing the Pig
146   R.S. Thomas — Song at the Year's Turning
147   Dannie Abse — Something Ending
147   Francis Kilvert — Braving the Snow Storm
148   Siân James — Grief
149   D. Parry-Jones — 'Dydd Calan'
151   Brenda Chamberlain — On Bardsey
152   John Davies — The Comeback
153   Tony Conran — Bethlehem
154   R.S. Thomas — Epiphany
154   Dannie Abse — Portrait of the Artist as a Middle-Aged Man

155   *Author's Acknowledgements*
156   *Publisher's Acknowledgements*

For Siân James, a valued friend

Introduction

Christmas is celebrated as keenly in Wales as anywhere and here for the first time is an anthology reflecting the Welsh experience of Christmas over the years, as seen by many of the country's leading writers.

Mass, the nativity play, the Mari Lwyd tradition, the celebratory meal, the gifts, the carols, and the turkey — trophy of the season — are among the subjects of poems, stories, diaries and letters written over the last century or more.

Naturally a large number of the items in this book are celebratory, and some of these are inextricably linked to the spiritual basis of the festival. The earliest writer represented is the seventeenth century poet Rowland Watkyns, who hails the nativity with these words:

> The Angels have sung the day, and so will I
> That have more reason to be glad than they

while the contemporary poet Ruth Bidgood rejoices at

> the birth of an eternal
> reason for hope.

In an essay, R.S. Thomas recalls a wartime Christmas Eve in rural Wales when 'one could believe Thomas Hardy's peasant in "The Oxen" that the beasts were kneeling'.

Eiluned Lewis describes a nineteenth century matins service in a Welsh cathedral where the singing of the choir '... those short-lived yet deathless voices, had invited the faithful people to come to Bethlehem.'

Also in a celebratory context we have Bruce Chatwin's

marvellous account of a nativity play from *On the Black Hill*, which did not go entirely according to plan. A teacher whose prompting failed to prevent fluffed lines 'called out "Curtain" and asked all present to sing "Once in Royal David's City"'.

In a letter Dylan Thomas muses on an uneventful Christmas Day at Cwmdonkin Drive in 1933 and concludes that one day he will tell any children he may have of '... the miracle of Christ and the devastating effect of too many nuts upon a young stomach'.

Custom is evoked in the form of the Mari Lwyd by Michael Gareth Llewelyn and Vernon Watkins; and is subverted by Richard Burton, who in his only short story, writes of political radicalism on Christmas Eve. Father Christmas is subjected to a gender change by Siân James and Stuart Nolan catalogues the ingredients of a truly adult Welsh Christmas: '3 bottles red wine. / 1 bottle white wine. / 6 cans lager'.

The Welsh Christmas is yearned for from abroad. Imprisoned in wartime Italy, Selyf Roberts is moved by the bells of Parma and reflects on the bells of Llandrillo-yn-Rhos which 'had been tied and were mute'. While far away in India, Alun Lewis puts his world in perspective by contemplating past Christmases.

Certain items have a specific geographical focus. These include recollections of childhood festivities in the Rhondda by Rhydwen Williams and Mary Davies Parnell, impressions of a far from happy wartime Christmas in Swansea by Denis Ratcliffe, D.J. Williams writing about 'a pagan custom' in Carmarthenshire, John Wain's fictional account of a Christmas in the hills of Gwynedd and John Idris Jones' description of a family get-together in the Berwyns.

On a Boxing Day pantomime trip we find the young Emlyn Williams proudly reflecting from his cheap seat 'we possessed a theatre, licensed by the Lord Chamberlain to the Welsh Family Williams'. While Dannie Abse approaches the panto clinically, diagnosing diseases in a number of characters: Cinderella is an hallucinating alcoholic, while Snow White has profound anaemia.

But Christmas is a time when unhappiness and grief can

assume a greater poignancy and this, too, is reflected in these pages. Francis Kilvert's account of the funeral service of Little Davie on Christmas Day 1878 never fails to move me with its reference to the bell chiming 'softly and slowly to greet the little pilgrim coming to his rest'. The widely disparate poets Bobi Jones and Ifor Thomas both write movingly of sickness at Christmas.

Other writers take an ironic, darkly comic view of the traditional happy Christmas and these include, predictably perhaps, Robert Minhinnick, Mike Jenkins and Peter Finch. Finch writes in a haiku with characteristic honesty:

> Nadolig heddwch
> Half of Wales don't care
> Other half can't pronounce it.

John Davies presents the Bethlehem stable as though it was a night club, with Jesus making a comeback. 'Can't beat Max Boyce though' comments one of the audience.

I can think of no better way of summing up than with the words of the incomparable Gwyn Thomas, who described Christmas as 'arising from a deep, dumb, sincere wanting on the part of a great mass of people.'

My aim has been to present vivid images of the iconography of Christmas as captured in both poetry and prose. If you, the reader, derive half the pleasure and interest which I experienced in compiling the book then I shall have achieved my objective.

Dewi Roberts

Advent to Christmas Eve

Hilary Llewellyn-Williams
Holly

July 8-August 4

Here in high summer, holly sets fruit
that will redden come Christmas.
Its prickles gloss and crackle in the sun.
Those deathless leaves make holly king.

This tree is holy, but not kind. What
is this holiness? What gift of grace
is so sharp-edged, dark-branched, hedged
with superstition, crowned with thorn?

Last summer's holly scratched my small
son as he climbed a bank, from rib
to breastbone a long stripe, with beads
of berry-blood, a flaxen Christ, arms up

and crying. This summer's rain
has blighted our best crops; but the trees
thrive, the trees take precedence. Green
under grey skies: reign of wood and water.

As the days shorten, holly's power grows:
ripening power, the birth power, power
from behind the eyes, dream power, spear-
leaved and bitter-barked and full of berries.

Holly saplings under graveyard yews
like prongs of resurrection, spring
from the shadows. The yews red-fleshed
and folded secretly, gave birth to them.

Blood mixed with soil was the old way
harvests grew fat, and holly ruled the feast.
My torn child heals: a ragged silver line
across his breast, fades as he flourishes.

Vernon Watkins
Midwinter

Midwinter: packed with ice the butt,
Splitting its sides.
Roots hard as iron; the back door shut.
Heaped wood a ringing axe divides.
Sacks on the pipes. No river flows,
No tap, no spring. A skater goes
Skimming across the pond. A stone
Stays on the ice where it is thrown.
Under a bone a blue-tit swings,
The keen light dancing on his wings.
To robins crusts and crumbs are tossed,
Yellow against the white of frost.
A quilted world. Glazed mistletoe.
Spades glint, and sledges glide, on snow.
Boys scroop it up with tingling hands,
Steadying the snowman where he stands,
Numb into dusk. Then holly boughs
Darken the walls in many a house,
While moth-flakes pile on wood and ground,
Muffling the panes, and hide all sound.
The tree of Winter, Winter's tree:
Winter a dark, a naked tree.

Gillian Clarke
Midwinter

The narrowest month and bitter cold.
The moment the house yawns awake
and Earth turns back from the black wastes
of space, dawn breaks in an amphora of blood.

We breakfast in our room of glass
to watch trees burn,
sky overflowing in a cup,
a grapefruit-half in a bowl of gold.

The children sip their juice and gaze
amazed at the gourd of candlefire,
the star in the East so beautiful
it could blind you — like God's eye.

Michael Gareth Llewelyn
An Old World Custom

Never were old world customs so much in evidence as with the approach of the Christmas season.

As soon as we had 'ducked apples' on '*Nos Cyn Gaeaf*', 'the night before winter' or All-Hallows Eve, we began to look forward to the coming of Christmas. We counted the days and wondered if it would be a white Christmas with snowballs and snowmen, a black-frost Christmas with sliding on the ponds, or a soft Christmas, mild from the westerly winds that blew over Swansea Bay and brought with them the soft fine rain.

> *Glaw mân Abertawe,*
> *Tra parith y dydd*
> *Fe parith ynte.*

> Fine rain from Swansea,
> As long as the day lasts
> So will it last,

said the weather seers, who seemed never to understand that we small boys wanted a Yuletide with all the joys of the Christmas card.

A week or so before the festival, the Mari Lwyd company would begin their rounds, a little apologetic at first like a blackbird with its first songs. But as the great day came nearer the wassailers became more confident and fuller of the spirit of the year in more senses than one. Their song became stronger and choral as new stalwarts joined the Mari Lwyd company. Practice was making perfect.

> *Dyma ni'n dywad,*
> *Gyfeillion diniwad,*
> *I ofyn cawn genad*
> *I ganu.*

> Here we come,
> Friends — without harm —
> To ask your permission
> To sing.

The quaint chant came along the breeze, over the green valley, from the farmhouses where the singers were trying out their voices. People at their cosy firesides would say, 'The Mari Lwyd is out, Christmas is upon us once more,' and they would smile at each other and talk of old times.

It meant nothing to these carollers that the Mari Lwyd was the remnant of an old mystery play depicting the flight to Egypt and which was only appropriate to Twelfth Night. To Welsh villagers the Mari Lwyd came at Christmas and persisted into the New Year, its song perhaps changed a little like the cuckoo's as new verses were added to the seemingly endless refrain.

When they came to our door, I would essay to compete with the *pwncwr* or impromptu librettist, who took up the challenge from outside. His uncomplimentary remarks in rhyme and song about my appearance, mentality and incompetence were usually so scathing that I was nonplussed very soon and, admitting defeat, the door was opened to the wassailers, to be regaled with cakes and rhubarb wine (ours was a temperance household!) and given a bright new shilling.

As they left they sang:

> *Ffarweliwch foneddigion,*
> *Ni gawsom groesaw ddigon.*

Bendith Duw f'o ar eich tai
A phob rhyw rhai o'ch dynion.

Farewell, gentlefolk.
We have received a warm welcome.
The Blessing of God be on your house
And upon all your people.

Vernon Watkins
from *The Ballad of the Mari Lwyd*

Bones of the dead should come on their knees
Under a pilgrim's cloak,
But out in the dark what devils are these
That have smelt our kitchen-smoke?
Listen. Listen. Who comes near?
What man with a price on his head?
What load of dice, what leak in the beer
Has pulled your steps from the dead?

Midnight. Midnight. Midnight. Midnight.
Hark at the hands of the clock.

'Starving we come from Gruffydd Bryn
And a great meal we have lost.
We might have stayed by the fire of the inn
Sheltered from the frost.
And there a sweet girl stood and spread
The table with good things,
Felinfoel beer with a mountain's head,
And a pheasant with hungry wings.'

Midnight. Midnight. Midnight. Midnight.
Hark at the hands of the clock.

'There were jumping sausages, roasting pies,
And long loaves in the bin,
And a stump of Caerphilly to rest our eyes,
And a barrel rolling in.
But dry as the grave from Gruffydd Bryn
We are come without one rest;
And now you must let our Mari in:
She must inspire your feast.'

Midnight. Midnight. Midnight. Midnight.
Hark at the hands of the clock.

'For She knows all from the birth of the Flood
To this moment where we stand
In a terrible frost that binds the blood
In a cramp that claws the hand.
Give us rhyme for rhyme through the wood of the door
Then open the door if you fail.
Our wit is come from the seawave's roar,
The stars, and the stinging hail.'

Midnight. Midnight. Midnight. Midnight.
Hark at the hands of the clock.

Go back. We have heard of dead men's bones
That hunger out in the air.
Jealous they break through their burial-stones,
Their white hands joined in a prayer.
They rip the seams of their proper white clothes
And with red throats parched for gin,
With buckled knuckles and bottle-necked oaths
They hammer the door of an inn.

Sinner and saint, sinner and saint:
A horse's head in the frost.

'O pity us, brothers, through snow and rain
We are come from Harlech's waves.

Tall spears were laid on the mountain.
We hid in the warriors' caves.
We were afraid when the sun went down,
When the stars flashed we were afraid;
But the small lights showed us Machynlleth town,
And bent on our knees we prayed.'

Midnight. Midnight. Midnight. Midnight.
Hark at the hands of the clock.

Though you come from the grim wave's monklike hood
And Harlech's bitter coast,
White horses need white horses' food:
We cannot feed a ghost.
Cast your Lwyd to the white spray's crest
That pounds and rides the air.
Why should we break our lucky feast
For the braying of a mare?

Ruth Bidgood
First Snow

In this pure winter theme
the year's unborn variations
lie warm and curled.
A maiden landscape mothers
the unforeseen.
Past winters remembered
cannot lessen the newness;
first snow is again and always
first of all snows.
There is no precedent
for this particular moment.
As if we have never before
hoped, we rake the sky

for a gentle omen of light
promising for this year,
this white valley,
the birth of an eternal
reason for hope.

Janet Dubé
Advent Poem for Jo

At Abergwen
the holly tree
is skirted
like bright dimity:

at Glangwili
the holly tree
is stately
in striped majesty:

in Llandysul
the holly tree
is pointed
like a Christmas tree:

and Abernawmor's
holly tree
beside the pond
for all to see;

a funny shape,
quite low and round,
thin branches ragged
to the ground

sings red and green
with treasure crowned:
the dearest tree
for miles around.

R.S. Thomas
The Qualities of Christmas

Christianity has tended to be transformed or adapted in every
country into which it has made its way. Perhaps the saddest
transformation here has been its increasing commercialization:
the rush, the false gaiety, the perfunctory exchange of cards
and presents; the colossal expenditure of energy and cash on
the wrong things. But the subtlest influence remains climatic;
and afterwards economic. Our more temperate winters afford
a dual approach. We can relish the coldness of the season, the
red cheeks, the high blood, without becoming insensitive to
the claims of the hungry bird at our window, the pathos of bare
boughs, and the darker associations of red berries in the snow.
Also our economic prosperity over many centuries built up a
feeling of snugness and warmth and good cheer within. 'Fire
and sleet and candlelight' — these lend zest to Christmas
indoors in a comfortable home, without blinding us to the
plight of the less fortunate without, those who are caught in
'the cauld, cauld blast'.

But there is something more. Christ was born in Bethlehem.
Bethlehem was a town. But all around lay the country. This
was the glory of the earlier towns. 'The dark, satanic mills' had
not arrived. The country came up to the town walls, as is so
evident in the paintings of the mediaeval and renaissance
masters. The place where Jesus was born was used as a cow
byre. The creatures were there with their hay-sweet breath and
their smell of the earth. And all around there was the country.
St Luke tells us: 'And in the same country there were shepherds abiding in the field, keeping watch over their flock by

night.' 'Abiding in the field.' What a sense of the surrounding country we get in those words! It is this sense of the harmony of town and country which is so much part of the Nativity. Mary, like a farm wife, comes into the town to give birth to her child. The town that is the summit of man's achievement, the city that he builds to the glory of God. And the shepherds come in from the fields to see this great wonder that has occurred, symbols of that flowing in of food and inspiration and re-invigoration without which all towns must wither and die. And there they find Christ, a sign of God's blessing upon the town as the focus of civilization; the place where the raw material of nature, of country districts around, is transformed into those higher things which are for the benefit and enrichment of all.

It should be so here and now. Despite our many towns and cities, we are country folk at heart. This is still a green island. Our memories of Christmas, our experiences of it, are country ones. If we cannot get to the country for Christmas, we import it into our homes. We hang up holly and mistletoe. We arrange flowers and ivy and yew. We bear in the Christmas tree and make it grow again in our houses. We bring out our store of nuts and apples, and dine off game and poultry that but a few days earlier were on a Scottish moor or a Welsh hillside. These are reminders of the country around, that abiding wildness and freshness, where the strange stillness and hush of Christmas Eve can best be appreciated.

I remember one Christmas Eve; I think it was in 1941. There were rumours that the Germans would attempt an airborne landing that night. The countryside where I lived was wrapped in a thick, damp fog. The lanes were empty. No light shone from the scattered farmsteads. The trees loomed up, windless and eerie, in the darkness. The silence was terrifying, the suspense intolerable. But it was suspense for the wrong thing. On other Christmas Eves I have walked up hill lanes to take a present of home-made cakes to a bedridden farmer. But how different the atmosphere! The air cold and clear, the ash trees bone-white against the sky. A friendly stream of warm light flowing from the farm window, and above, the shrill harness of the stars. And if a fox barked, it was a merry sound, for on such a Christmas Eve one could believe with Thomas Hardy's peasant in 'The Oxen' that all the beasts were kneeling.

> Christmas Eve, and twelve of the clock
> 'Now they are all on their knees'

Hardy ends his poem on a characteristic note, half cynical, half wistful:

> I should go with him in the gloom,
> Hoping it might be so.

'Hoping it might be so'! But it is so.

Peter Finch
Some Christmas Haiku

On the moors
The snow caught by grass
No one to see it

Not Christmas holy silent night
But the holiday season
Above the cloud same old moon

Cinio Nadolig
Boldy praising Iesu
Menu's in English

In the chapel
Old wood
After so many years still shining

Through the dense firs
Light of a wrecked car
Burning

Early snow
On the berried holly
Some cretin starts complaining

Old man
Pulling crackers by himself
Sound clear to the big dipper

Sound of retching
Three men in an empty street
Crushing lager cans

Street guitarist mangles carols
On the shopkeeper's face
The shopkeeper's mask

Gwyn Thomas
Scrooge, A Defence

In brooding about Christmas I never failed to find Scrooge a sympathetic figure. Not Scrooge as a thrift worshipper, a curmudgeon. Him I could willingly drop in the Thames. But Scrooge as a man who is fairly pleased with the day-to-day pattern of his existence and who, at Christmas, feels that his sanity is threatened.

It would not be possible to fix the percentage of Scrooges in any given Christmas population. I have a feeling that Dickens gave the old miser such a vindictive birching and treated those dim Cratchitts to such a buttering-up, that the average Scrooge now feels it advisable to duck out of the way for the duration of the feast to wait for the first full-scale bursting of water pipes in the New Year before smiling again and telling us that he told us so.

I would say that one could find ten million people in our land who are not at ease about Christmas; who deplore its gluttony, its glutinous sentimentality, its way of accelerating the transmission of viruses at the sight of mistletoe, its horrific puddings and the tigerish exploitation by business interests of some very charming impulses of love and tenderness. But of those ten million people you would need a strong-arm squad to persuade even twenty of them to come together and work for practical reforms to make the occasion a little less vulgar and meretricious. The modern Christmas, like that other incredible modern phenomenon, the Butlin holiday camp, arises from a well of deep, dumb, sincere wanting on the part of a great mass of people. If there were no Christmas as we know it today we can be sure that we would waste no time in finding some other seasonal excuse for an avalanche of dead poultry and a blizzard of greetings. Humans need a moment of excess, of irrational affection for the whole species. That is the miracle of Christmas; that the species can feel fond of itself for even hours on end.

I am solidly for it. As the Welsh eisteddfod bard once said about sex: 'if there's nothing you can do to break its hold, just join in quietly and wait until people get tired'. I cherish every moment of daft gaiety it generates though my gorge still rises somewhat at paper hats and cracker mottoes. I would like the Yule-tide essence to be dyked, piped and suffused into every corner of the year where time and spirit tend to go slow and grey.

To this end I would even join the dedicated dervishes who throng the hotel floors on Christmas Eve bringing life to the boil, and I would doff my customary dun velour to whoop it up in a tricorne of multicoloured tissue. I might even buy a box of crackers just for the moral advice. And I want all the Scrooges, declared or not, to be in the act. I do not want a sudden conversion within a few days of Christmas. I want no truck with sudden spasms of compassion induced by the Dickensian dodge of startling them into remorse or fear with the phantoms of Past, Present and Future. I would like them, some time during January, to become aware of the dignity and needs of others, to observe the spots where life might have become scuffed and deplorable, and to work up to a peak of benevolence in the year's last month. Having stood in the clouds to make that appeal I now come down to have my head defrosted.

Ruth Bidgood
Magpies at Christmas

Robins are back on the cards
this year; so is a whole
peace-conference of doves, white on blue,
on silver, on martial red. Now, out there,
just below the window, come
sturdy Christmas beggars, two
conniving magpies, picking and scraping
at the cats' plate, conversing
or congratulating themselves
in surprisingly gentle cheeps and coos,
and in their greed oblivious of me,
till at some minuscule movement
they register shock, tilt heads, fly.

Douglas Phillips
Christmas at Pentrepoeth School, Carmarthen
(Demolished to make way for a car park)

Each year as the gas lamps susurrussed
The magic lantern beamed,
A box of flicks with painted windows of wonder.

Through the chalk-dust motes,
Gleaming like tiny galaxies,
The bright bulb shone, a mid-winter sun,
Its phases haloing the frescoed screen.

Like stilted apparitions the pictures wobbled into
        focus:
Scrooge hunched over skinflint ledgers,
Bob Cratchitt pelting home, with blizzarding comforter,
And, to a hiss of tightening breath,
The ghastly, ghostly face upon the door.

In stiff progression, the tableaux jerked:
A phantom Marley, padlocked to his tail of purses,
The spirits of Christmas, Past, Present,
And the black-palled spectre of Yet-to-Come,
A sombre basso-profundo doom
Until the piping treble
Of Tiny Tim's triumph.

Later, as the small hail scuttered
Against the window pane,
We practised our carols:
The tall brick building
Full, like a giant gingerbread house,
Of Hansels and Gretels chanting epiphanies,
With no witch croning to broomstick away their joy.

The children are gone now, the rooms long empty.
Only ghosts remain,

Invisible, except to the inner projectors
Of memory

Now, as the holly season approaches,
I walk down Orchard Street
Which blossomed daily with laughter ripening
On bobbing apple cheeks.
Far off the bells chant and the children chime,
But the playground is bare,
The classrooms are deaf,
And the opaque screens of the once-bright windows
    are blind.

Glyn Jones
Pugh, the Festive Policeman

Nobody who knew Rhysie seemed to trust him, and that night
we had to sleep in the same room as our auntie. She had hung
a white bed-sheet across the middle and we could see her
shadow undressing on it by the light of her candle. In the
morning Rhysie woke up first and because he didn't have
anything to do he started to cut my hair with our auntie's
scissors. He had a row for that when he got into the kitchen
but he was used to it.

   Our auntie put him into the spare clothes my mother had
packed for me in my cardboard case and bundled us both off
to school in the village. Everything was still thick with snow,
the scene on the way was pretty, but we were cold. The school
was small with only two teachers, and the headmaster was
giving the children their Christmas examination. He was a very
thick short man with little arms and legs, and over his big bald
head he had a few tails of wavy bright yellow hair like flat
unravelled rope. Rhysie and I sat in the same desk in the front
row and he asked us questions about Saint Nicholas in a big
voice. We couldn't answer any of them but he didn't give us a

row. Instead he started to sing 'While shepherds watched' loud enough to deafen you, banging like mad on the school piano at the same time. When he finished all the children clapped.

In the playground a boy called Bazzo shouted, 'Dunce' after Rhysie. Rhysie punched him in the chest and the ribs and clipped him across the side of the head. The boy tied to kick him on the thigh and Rhysie closed with him. They fell to the ground struggling and rolling about in the wet snow and soon the boy began to cry because Rhysie was beating him. When I pulled Rhysie off there were two purple sets of teeth marks in his cheeks, perfect, where Bazzo had bitten him twice. That night after tea, when our auntie was doing a bit of extra washing, a woman called at the back door and complained that Rhysie had nearly murdered her boy. Auntie Kezia believed her and Rhysie went to bed without any supper.

Rhysie didn't like exams so the next day he got me to mitch. We went down the main road and spent our time throwing snowballs at the white stone-ginger bottles holding the wires on the telegraph poles. There were stones inside the snowballs. That night Pugh the policeman called in at our auntie's about it and she began to look more worried than ever. She was a small woman, her face yellow as a canary, and she had pale blue eyes always swimming about in a lot of water; she looked as though her eyeballs were slowly dissolving with anxiety.

Rhysie and I didn't like this Pugh at all. He was the shortest policeman we had ever seen, and the fattest, and he couldn't see properly without his glasses. If you watched him from the side standing on the front doorstep in his street you would notice that a lot of him was hanging out over the pavement. He had a big curving moustache and a red face the colour of an old roof, with the nose-part vanished, and half a dozen bottom teeth that stood up brown and rotten like a few old clay pipes in the fairground shooting gallery. He was very bossy and if he saw you kicking your cap up the street he would shout at you to stop it. And even if the village people left their ash-boxes outside a bit too long in the morning he would knock at the door and tell them to take them in.

The third day was the Christmas party in the church vestry

for the village children. Rhysie coaxed our auntie to let us go, although I didn't want to much because of the mess Rhysie had made of my hair. The vestry was a very small low building built all of dark brown wood. For the party it was decorated with streamers and balloons, and crowds of kids from the village were screaming and running about the place in their best clothes. Rhysie and I had a good tea by ourselves after all the others had finished and as we were eating it a tall man came and talked to us. We thought he must be the vicar. His thick loaf-coloured hair was parted deep down the middle, it looked like the cut in a crust of bread. He asked us who we were and when we told him he shot up one of his eyebrows into his hair, pulled it down quickly, and then went away.

After tea all the gaslights in the vestry were turned out and the place was in darkness except for the little candles alight on the Christmas tree. The vicar told us all to be quiet and to look up at the roof at the place he was pointing to, just above the tree. We saw the wooden manhole in the ceiling taken away and a face, with glasses on and a big white beard, showed in the square hole, looking down at us. It was Santa Claus. A ladder was fetched and after a big struggle he began to climb down into the vestry in his hood and his red robes. Some of the little children screamed when they saw him, but Rhysie and I knew him by his boots and his big bum, we could see it was old Pugh the policeman.

Siân James
Mother Christmas

At Christmas there was a special concert when all the chapel children, even those from down Mill Bank who'd only started coming to Sunday School at the beginning of December, had a present from the Christmas tree.

In spite of the war, we had good presents, but our Father Christmas was always a hopeless failure, a mumbling old man with a slipping beard, that no one, not even the babies in Class 1, believed in.

Jenny Williams changed all that. One year, she came on in a little red cloak and bonnet. 'I'm Mother Christmas,' she said. 'My old man's been called up. Yes, he's gone from under my feet. Good job, too. He was always an old nuisance. And mean. Ooo. He used to spend more on those dirty old reindeers than he did on me. Did you think he'd bought you those presents last year? No, it was the Ladies Sewing Circle. All he ever did was show off in his red suit. And that beard. It wasn't real. No. Did you think it was real? Of course you didn't.'

Mother Christmas was a huge success.

R.S. Thomas
Carol

What is Christmas without
snow? We need it
as bread of a cold
climate, ermine to trim

our sins with, a brief
sleeve for charity's
scarecrow to wear its heart
on, bold as a robin.

Bruce Chatwin
The Nativity Play

... it was freezing. A pair of paraffin stoves did nothing to heat the benches at the back. A draught whined in under the door, and the floorboards reeked of disinfectant. The audience sat muffled in scarves and overcoats. The preacher, a missionary returned from Africa, shook hands with each member of his flock.

Drawn across the stage was a curtain consisting of three grey ex-Army blankets, peppered with moth holes.

Mrs Redpath rejoined her uncles. The lights were switched off, except for the light onstage. From behind the curtain they heard the whispering of children.

The schoolteacher slipped through the curtain and sat down at the piano-stool. Her knitted hat was the same puce pink as the azalea on the piano; and as her fingers hammered the keyboard, the hat bobbed up and down, and the petals of the azalea quivered.

'Carol Number One,' she announced. '"O Little Town of Bethlehem" — which will be sung by the children only.'

After the opening bars, the sound of faltering trebles drifted over the curtain; and through the moth-holes, the twins saw flashes of sparkling silver, which were the tinsel haloes of the angels.

The carol ended, and a blonde girl came out front, shivering in a white nightie. In her diadem there was a silver-paper star.

'I am the star of Bethlehem....' Her teeth chattered. ''Tis ten thousand years since God put a great star in the sky. I am that star....'

She finished the prologue. Then the curtain jerked back with the noise of squeaky pulleys to reveal the Virgin Mary, in blue, on a red rubber kneeler, scrubbing the floor of her house in Nazareth. The Angel Gabriel stood beside her.

'I am the Angel Gabriel,' he said in a suffocated voice. 'And I have come to tell you that you are going to have a baby.'

'Oh!' said the Virgin Mary, blushing crimson. 'Thank you very much, sir!' But the Angel fluffed the next line, and Mary fluffed the one after, and they both stood helplessly in the middle of the stage.

The teacher tried to prompt them. Then, seeing that no amount of prompting could rescue the scene, she called out, 'Curtain!' and asked all present to sing 'Once in Royal David's City'.

Everyone knew the words without having to open their hymnals. And when the curtain drew back again, everyone guffawed at the two-piece donkey that kicked and bucked and neighed and nodded his papier-mâché head. Two scene-shifters carried in a bale of straw, and a manger for feeding calves.

'That's my Kevin!' whispered Mrs Redpath, nudging Benjamin in the ribs.

A little boy had come onstage in a green tartan dressing-gown. Wound round his head was an orange towel. He had a black beard gummed to his chin.

The twins sat up and craned their necks; but instead of facing the audience, Father Joseph shied away and spoke his lines to the backdrop: 'Can't you find us a room, sir! My wife's going to have a baby at any minute.'

'I ain't got a room in the place,' replied Reuben the innkeeper. 'The whole town's chock-a-block with folks as come to pay their taxes. Blame the Roman Government, not me!

'I got this stable, though,' he went on, pointing to the manger. 'You can sleep in there if you want to.'

'Oh, thanks very much, sir!' said the Virgin, brightly. 'It'll do very nicely for humble folks like us.'

She started rearranging the straw. Joseph still stood facing the backdrop. He raised his right arm stiffly to the sky.

'Mary!' he shouted, suddenly plucking up courage. 'I can see something up there! Looks like a cross to me!'

'A cross? Ugh! Don't mention that word. It reminds me of Caesar Augustus!'

Through the double thickness of their corduroys, Lewis could feel his brother's kneecap, shaking: for Father Joseph had spun round, and was smiling in their direction.

'Yes,' said the Virgin Mary towards the end of the final scene. 'I think it's the loveliest baby I ever set eyes on.'

As for the Jones twins, they too, were in Bethlehem. But it was not the plastic doll that they saw. Nor the innkeeper, nor the shepherds. Nor the papier-mâché donkey, nor the living sheep that nibbled at the straw. Nor Melchior with his box of chocolates. Nor Kaspar with his bottle of shampoo. Nor Black

Balthazar with his crown of red cellophane and a ginger jar. Nor the Cherubim and Seraphim, nor Gabriel, nor the Virgin Mary herself. All they saw was an oval face with grave eyes and a fringe of black hair beneath a wash-towel turban. And when the choir of angels started singing, 'We will rock you, rock you, ro-ock you...' they rocked their heads in time and tears dripped on to their watch-chains.

Tony Curtis
The Infants' Christmas Concert

A moment of hush, held breath —
the fairies and robbers, the soldiers
and dancers are in position
— then the piano begins.
This sounds otherworldly,
each note a drop of water falling distantly.

Angels swallow trumpets,
a robot trips and turtles in his cardboard shell;
the ballerina crumples and cries.
They may not know why, but still
perform for us the pattern of sentiment,
superstition and love: we sigh,
smile, laugh and applaud.

'The Rich man gave them a bag of gold
and everyone cheered on the day
the church had a new bell.'
The couple are starched in best white —
as the singing swells, they marry
and claim their gold.
It is intensely sad and fleetingly
realises the ghosts of our innocence.

Flashlights — the year's frozen
for this instant.
Keep that — don't move — stay there,
stay somewhere like that forever.

It all builds to The Nativity:
Joseph, Mary and the three glittering Kings
change without age, time after time.
Only the baby Jesus doll remains,
a scarred and worn wooden face held magically
fresh each year in the laundered swaddling.
The audience — parents and children in arms,
grandparents and neighbours, point and giggle,
there's a glow and, finally, we all sing.

This has worked some sort of renewal,
some sort of ending.

Herbert Williams
Billy Scrooge and the Santagram

I can't remember now who first called him Billy Scrooge, but
the name suited him and it stuck. He thought it a bit of a
compliment in a way, because he hated Christmas so much.

He'd come down from North Wales, can't remember when
exactly, after living in one of them little quarrying villages near
Caernarfon. At least there used to be quarries there but I
suppose by now they've gone the same way as the pits.

Let's get this straight right away, he wasn't a bad bloke at all.
Talked in a nasal whine but they all do that in North Wales,
don't they? Must be something in the air, I suppose.

Now, Billy Scrooge was a good worker — a shotfirer in the
pit. And he wasn't mean neither, not in the ordinary way of
things. Stood his round and gave his bit to good causes with
the best. It's just that he hated Christmas, that's all.

Hated? The word isn't strong enough. He loathed and despised it — all of it! Christmas cards with chubby robins, canned carols blaring away, lit-up trees stuck in front windows, Santa Clauses in the big stores — he hated them most of all.

'What about the Christmas message?' someone piped up once, out of devilment. 'Not against that are you?'

'The only message I know,' said Billy, quick as a flash, 'is keep your face out of trouble and your hands in your pockets.'

Well, as I say, nobody minded Billy so he went his own way and we went ours. Until old Bagsy Turner came to live in our village, that is. I don't know how he came to be called Bagsy so don't ask. But the long and short of it is that he didn't like Billy Scrooge one little bit.

'Tell you what we'll do,' he said, a week or two before Christmas. 'We'll have a Santagram for Billy. You know, one of them girls who dress up and take the mick out of people.'

'What's the point of that?' asked Ned Price, who prided himself on his fairness. 'Billy Scrooge don't do no harm to no-one.'

'It's only a joke, mun,' protested Bagsy, with a hurt look. 'Nobody's going to take exception to that, are they? Christmas, innit?' But we knew it wasn't just a joke to Bagsy, because there was a nasty side to that bloke. You could see it in the way he looked at you, all mean and sly.

Slowly, though, we weakened. To tell you the truth, we could all do with a bit of cheering up at that time, what with the pits closing down and the UB40s flying around like confetti. And the idea of a female Santa tickled us pink. It was something to take the edge off that miserable feeling in our gut.

The trouble is, when the big night arrived there was two foot of snow in our village. 'No-one can get through this lot,' moaned Des Whitfield, who made a right meal of bad news. 'The roads are blocked for miles. They give it out on the telly.'

But we all turned up at The Fountain just the same. And so did Billy, all unsuspecting.

Then suddenly in she came. With her big white beard and bright red cloak, large as life. She made a beeline for Billy and sent him up something rotten, reciting comic verses and all that and kissing him under the mistletoe. She worked hard, fair play. And a trimmer Santa you never saw.

Well, there we were enjoying every minute of it when out she marched, dragging Billy after her. It happened so fast we were stuck to our seats in surprise. Then out we all rushed — but not a sight did we see of them anywhere.

'Well, I'll be blowed,' said Ben Jones. 'He's got off with her good and proper. But where the 'ell have they gone?'

Next day Billy Scrooge was back — propping up the bar, large as life. With the biggest smile on his face you've ever seen in all your born days. 'Happy Christmas, boys,' he said. 'Pints all round!'

Then in came Bagsy Turner, white as a ghost. 'Just had a call from the Santagram people,' he whispered. 'Apologising for last night. Said they couldn't get through the snow for love nor money.'

I looked at him. He looked at me. We both looked at Billy.

He's a different bloke now. Loves Christmas, every minute of it. And laughs like a drain when he sees them Santa Clauses in the shops. It's as if he knows something about Father Christmas we don't. Know what I mean?

Idris Davies
A Star In The East

When Christmastide to Rhymney came
    And I was six or seven
I thought the stars in the eastern sky
    Were the brightest stars of heaven.

I chose the star that glittered most
    To the east of Rhymney town
To be the star above the byre
    Where Mary's babe lay down.

And nineteen hundred years would meet
Beneath a magic light,
And Rhymney share with Bethlehem
A star on Christmas night.

Eiluned Lewis
A Sad Dark Tune

Outside in the dark the dogs have started barking, and from
somewhere far away in the house there is the sound of voices
and opening doors; then down the passage they hear —

'Children, children! Come quick and listen! The carol-singers
are here!' and they rush out of the nursery, pell-mell, before
Louisa can get at them with brush and comb or mention of
clean pinafores — for this is Christmas Eve and the carol-singers
have come to sing in the hall.

They came in, scraping their feet and clearing their throats,
and stood in a circle under the swinging lamp, facing inwards,
their eyes fixed on their leader, Mr Jenkins the Shoes. Lucy sat
on the bend of the stairs from where she could see the wave in
Johnny Dowster's hair, the gap in Bill Morgan's front teeth
and the way the lump in Mr Elias Jones's throat worked up
and down when he sang. Mr Jenkins gave the signal and they
began, very softly at first.

See amid the winter's snow,
Born for us on Earth below;
See the tender lamb appears
Promised from eternal years.

Lucy was not sure whether they meant Jesus or the first forlorn
little lamb that would soon be born in the winter fields. The
two grew confused in her mind: she knew only that it was
something young and tender which had braved the cold and
harshness of the world, something which might be hurt if she

did not do something to help it, if she did not wrap it safely in her arms.

The carol ended; they were consulting together as to what they should sing next. Lucy wished they would sing for ever and that she might sit there safe in the shadow, smelling the pungent scent of the bruised ivy leaves hanging round the lamp. Now they were singing about the ivy:

> The holly and the ivy now both are full well grown,
> Of all the trees that spring in wood the holly bears
>   the crown;
> The holly bears a blossom as white as lily flower,
> And Mary bore sweet Jesus, to be our sweet Saviour.
>
> The holly bears a berry as red as any blood,
> And Mary bore sweet Jesus, to make poor sinners
>   good;
> The holly bears a prickle as sharp as any thorn,
> And Mary bore sweet Jesus on Christmas day in
>   the morn.

It was a sad, dark tune, and now Lucy understood that nothing she could do would keep the little lamb of God from being hurt. How cold it had grown suddenly! They had all lost their way in the dark wood, and the sharp leaves of the holly were wet with blood.

'Lucy,' her mother called, 'why are you hiding up there? Come down and help pass round the mince-pies.'

So it was all right, after all. She came slowly down the stairs, shook hands with the carol-singers and handed round the dish of pies. They smelt warm and spicy and she and Delia were told they might each have one for supper. Lucy climbed on her father's knee and rubbed her cheek against the roughness of his tweed coat. She felt deliciously drowsy — the terror of darkness and the cruel, bleeding holly leaves quite forgotten. To-morrow was Christmas day; to-night they would hang up their stockings.

Peter Finch
More Christmas Haiku

Ice sky above B&Q
Cut fir trees burn
In the breath of customers

Tinsel blows across the car park
In the supermarket
Someone steals a chicken

can't couldn't
then snow
somehow

Outside the building society
A man in a Santa suit
And three women smoking

In the Christmas cold
So drunk she can't
Find her car

Facing the void
of Christmas
burning twigs

Nadolig heddwch
half of Wales don't care
Other half can't pronounce it.

Kate Roberts
The Battle of Christmas

Sunday, December 1

There's one thing to be said for a poor sermon, you can let your mind wander where you will, and my mind was in the cellar throughout the sermon tonight, with the scores of toys that were waiting to come out of their shavings tomorrow, be carried up to the shop and placed on the shelves. Talk about a snail! Every other shop in town did that a fortnight ago. And I've been putting it off as long as I could because I'm afraid of a battle, and Christmas is a battle to me now. Another task will be to move the poll-parrot from the shop and try to keep him quiet in the kitchen. I came close to losing all my business because of him last year: it became a howling bedlam after I spoke my mind to a great lady from here in town when she came to buy English-language Christmas cards and said that the poetry in them wasn't classical enough. Polly cursed her ancestors back to Adam.

Decided to enjoy every bite of my supper tonight, for fear I won't have any appetite for food again before my Christmas dinner. Decided that I'm a coward, when I'm afraid of a little thing like a rush. Envied Lloyd the School who's been retired for years.

Meg made an omelet for supper instead of the eternal cold meat, frying potatoes with it and putting onion juice with them. Ate it all slowly and chewed every morsel twice. The trifle slipped down my throat like flummery. 'Stop sighing,' Meg said, 'you won't shorten tomorrow by sighing.' Enjoyed a smoke before going to bed. Dreamt I was smothering in the dust and the shavings.

translated by Joseph P. Clancy

Gwyn Thomas
Lifting the Curse of Shabbiness

... it was the Christmas Eve singing that brought the full enchantment and lifted the curse of shabbiness and inadequacy that might otherwise have settled us for life. The local male voice choir, a platoon that could produce more serene and satin sounds than I have heard since, backed by the Jubilee Silver and Brass band, would move through the town in the hours before midnight. They were flanked by a dozen or so of us boys from the Band of Hope Junior Operatic group — a clutch of brazen thrushes. We bore storm lanterns on poles and occasionally added to the treble and alto lines with voices that gave the note of innocence essential to these occasions.

This was not the casual mercenary type of carolling which is content with braying 'God Rest Ye Merry' at a street corner then taking the collection box up and down the street. Oh no. This was purely an act of giving. We played and sang only before the houses of the lonely, the deprived and the sick. These were chosen in advance by the secretary of the Welfare Institute. He was a man sensitive to life's anguish almost to the point of madness. However placid and genial life might seem to us, to him the tragic sense was pacing like a leopard just beneath.

Even if you were guffawing with a genuine awareness of life's vigorous absurdity, he would caution you to take it easy because you were now showing symptoms of morbid hysteria, and it was only a matter of days before you were trussed and trundled off to Bedlam. He had everybody tagged as a victim. He saw everybody in the town as stranded in some dark, yearning solitude. So there was scarcely a family not attended to on our Christmas Eve pilgrimage. We shuffled virtuously from house to house and there was barely more than a ten-second break between carols.

Often a tenant would come out and ask in a most jolly voice in what category of doom the secretary of the institute was putting him this year. At the end of each carol we boys would take gifts of fruit and nuts into the houses and the householders in turn would pour out a fair peg of vegetable wine for all who wanted it. Down went the stoups of parsnip, turnip and elderberry moonshine — stuff that had been fermenting for years and carried a wallop strong enough to blow a pantry wall into the garden of the house next door. There were stories of vintners still hanging on to their jars as they cleared the wall. By the time the night was ended men who for years had been steeped in austere and monkish habits would be flaring with resurgent desires, walking with the strutting puissance of Louis the Fourteenth, banging on the doors of old lovers, chasing girls up side-streets and playing havoc with the tempo of the carols.

We lads with the lanterns would be manipulating our poles like anglers to play a maximum of light on the sheet music of the less steady performers. Posses of calmer carollers would be sent out to bring the revellers to heel. They would be forced to stand and sing or play the sadder and more poignant type of carol. They would weep and the tears bore away the fever of self-renewal induced by the wine, the music, the illusion of creating the light of a new benediction through all the nights of the world. Our midnight journey would end on the town square. The police constable would tap his helmet, partly to spur us to a closure, partly to give us the beat for his favourite carol. We would sing it, for the joyous and loved as well as for the sad and the alone, our lanterns dipped in salutation to gentleness and pity. 'Tenderly sleeping, so tranquil and sweet, Jesus the loving and kind ....'

Kate Roberts
Pricking the Bubble

The two of them set out, wrapped to the nose like a roly poly, clogs on their feet and big scarves round their heads. The snow had drifted up the sides of the fire. The wind blew everywhere, down the chimney to lift the sacking on the hearth, under the front door, from the back. Their teeth chattered, and they felt as if the scarves were still tied round their heads. Soon, the peat began to blaze, and Nanw Siôn moved some more turves towards it and put a lump of coal in the eye of the fire. The smell of stew came from a saucepan on the hob. Nanw fetched three bowls and put them on the small white round table, cut some bread into them, and ladled out some stew with a cup.

'Now then, fill those stomachs of yours. It will warm you better than a drink of tea.'

She was right. Soon, the warmth crept into their feet and hands and ears. She poked the fire, and sparks flew up from beneath the turf and flame rose over it, and she turned up the wick of the lamp. The heat of the fire and the lamplight made everything look cosy, and the children grew drowsy. Nanw's nose was running, and she wiped it with a handkerchief made out of a flour bag and kept tucked under her apron strings. She wore a tweed shawl fastened over her shoulders with a big safety pin. Silence fell upon the kitchen, broken only by the purring of the cat, the clock ticking, the children snoring, Nanw breathing like a squeaky bellows, and an occasional crack from the fire.

Rhys woke up.

'What's tight with you?' he asked Nanw.

'Tight? What do you mean?' she asked.

'Mother said things were pretty tight with you.'

Begw dug him in the ribs.

'Well, they are ... life is pretty hard, but it always has been. Doesn't matter how much you get, you can't make both ends meet.'

'Mother has sent you a few things for Christmas,' said Begw.

'I gave the toffees,' said Rhys.

'I don't doubt you gave it a turn or two with the spoon,' said Nanw.

The basket was unpacked, Nanw saying, 'Well, well, well,' as each gift came out. 'Isn't she the kindest creature ever was.'

'We're going to have an old fashioned Christmas,' said Rhys.

Nanw looked at him as if he were mad.

'Who said so?'

'Begw.'

'What does she know about it?'

'Well, it's like this, Nanw Siôn. Every year I get Christmas cards with pictures of snow and holly and a little girl going through the snow with a bonnet and cape.'

'And you think it's you?'

'We've never had snow at Christmas before.'

'Nor have I, for that matter. It's all lies, this old fashioned Christmas.'

The children's faces fell.

'Why do they say so on the Christmas cards?'

'You'll learn some day that it's the people who tell most lies who make their fortunes quickest.'

Begw had nothing to say. She had been deceived for years, thinking of the wonderful world of long ago where Christmas was always white. At last she ventured to speak.

'Anyway their lies have come true this time, and perhaps it's now that the old fashioned Christmases are beginning.'

'Don't bother your head with such things, child. That's the way to end up in the Asylum.'

Rhys was lost. 'Never mind about those Christmas cards, they're silly things anyway. I like the real snow better,' he said.

'You've got it now, my boy. If you were as old as I am, living on the top of a mountain, you wouldn't want it. It ties you up. Here I am ... can't move a step, and I can't come down tomorrow to have dinner with you as usual.'

Rhys nearly cried. 'Do try and come,' he said.

'Try? Try? An old woman like me? What if I fell and broke my leg? No, I've got to stay here with the mice and the spiders.'

'And the cat,' said Begw, unkindly.

Anger blazed in Nanw Siôn's eyes.

'Do you know what it means to be lonely? No one to say a word to you, kind or unkind. Living with your own thoughts, that's what it is, for a woman like me, for the cat and the mice can't speak to you ....'

'Why don't you get a parrot?' asked Begw.

'Parrot? I'll parrot you, you cheeky little thing. Pity Rhys didn't stay at home and leave you to come by yourself through the snow, and then you'd know what loneliness is like.'

'That's what I'd like.'

'Sure enough you'd like it if the devil picked you up on his horns and tossed you down into the quarry.'

Begw laughed, but Rhys shuddered. He wanted to escape, but Nanw held him spellbound.

'And what's more, I don't want the cat to catch the mice. They keep me company. And the cat sleeps in the bedroom so that I can hear someone breathing. I like to hear the spiders ticking, although it's a sign of death. Death hasn't come my way yet.'

Rhys began to cry. He was sorry he had come, for this was a waking nightmare. Nanw Siôn relented somewhat.

'Don't cry, lad. Christmas will go by, like everything else. Nothing lasts long, grief or joy. I'll be down again to see your Mother and talk to her and turn the handle of the churn. She's the kindest woman in the world. I don't know who this girl belongs to. Don't forget to thank her for all these things.'

When they got out, the moon had risen, and the countryside looked as if someone had spread a white tablecloth over it. Rhys felt sorry for Nanw Siôn, all alone up there over Christmas, and even Begw began to think that a white Christmas was not so wonderful, after all. Much less romantic than when she set out on the journey. Nanw Siôn had pricked the bubble of an old fashioned Christmas ....

translated by Wyn Griffith

Gwyn Thomas
Ogley the Abstainer

... We had persuaded Ogley to join our Male Voice Choir, the Orpheans, to see if the laying on of heavy harmonies would stabilize his impulses. He joined, stipulating that he would add his voice only when the libretto of the piece we were singing dealt singly with death or deprivation, and it was good to see him during our rendering of such an item as 'The Jolly Roger' which stressed a love of rum and license. He would purse his lips so tightly he slowed down the vocal rate of the six singers next to him.

On that Christmas Eve the Orpheans, flanked by members of the Meadow Prospect Jubilee Band, shuffled out on their usual pilgrimage through the thin snow. The conductor of the Jubilee band, Elmo Lucroft, was more imperious than usual, wearing a tall black fur cap that he had received from a cousin of his who was engaged in some missionary work in Alaska. To respect the associations of this hat Elmo had warned his bandsmen to take no drink before starting, and Ogley Floyd, among the second tenors of the Orpheans and holding a lantern, was overjoyed to see the bandsmen shiver and shake as their mouths came into contact with their instruments, especially the euphonium player, a naturally chilly and doomed-looking voter, Bleddyn Bibey the Blast, who was surrounded by about a mile of cold pipe.

As part of our programme of chiding the life-force we stopped in front of houses of the sick, the lonely and the bereaved to take from the air the sting of their ache and loss. And at other houses we were invited in. We were all offered glasses of vegetable wine. Ogley stood aloof until we bombarded him with such cries as 'Only the wine from the fruit is wicked, Og. This stuff is made from such homely and trustworthy articles as parsnip and swede. Very harmless, though warming and tonic. All they do is take the chill off the stomach.' Ogley took a sip, saying: 'Just for the stomach, mark you. There is a touch of frost down there. I was pressed against a lamp-post when we did "Holy Night" in that last street.'

Ogley downed his first glass and became an enthusiast for the clean innocuous flavour of the stuff. He must have had a dozen helpings, winding up with that special parsnip of my father's which could have been used directly on quarry faces. We got back to Meadow Prospect square about eleven. Ogley's face was flushed and his eyes were blazing in a way that had that very touchy bass-drummer, Teifion Tamplin the Tattoo, keeping his sticks at the ready.

Then there was a low moaning from Ogley. At first we

thought it was Bibey blowing away out of habit, but then we saw that Ogley's neuroses were drawing their long firm corks and his urges were casting aside their cowl with the loudest cheer since the last war's end. That very attractive woman, Miss Catherine Ann Bottomley, who was an usherette in the Colisseum, came out of a side lane, and at the sight of her Ogley gave out some kind of jungle cry which we thought had been outlawed in the fringe after the first revival. He gave chase to Miss Bottomley, running like a stag but leaving the pavement too often for real speed.

Miss Bottomley, whose legs had developed like steel after years of marching up and down aisles, outstripped him, and then Ogley started out in pursuit of two maidens who were coming home from a dance. Our policeman, Leyshon the Law, came into view just as Willie Silicox was assigning various members of the Orpheans to start galloping off into the roads that fed the square giving out cries of desire and slogans directed against the years of quietness and restraint, all to create bits of diversionary chaos in which we could get Ogley back to normal. Leyshon made a long statement in which he said he had always been certain that the radical flank of the Orpheans would one day try to discredit Christmas and denounce Claus as a charlatan who was trying to concentrate the species' lust for kindliness into a single night and with his oblique approach from the roof to fox the voters who had had quite enough of misdirection. In the meantime we got hold of Ogley, held his head against the coldest wall in Meadow Prospect, read a series of chilling texts from the good Book and half drowned him in cocoa of the most austere tint made by Tasso while we got Theo Morgan the Monologue, that prince of reciters, to recite to him that fine temperance poem 'There's A Lurching Shadow On The Blind Tonight'.

Gillian Clarke
Snow

The dreamed Christmas,
flakes shaken out of silences so far
and starry we can't sleep for listening
for papery rustles out there in the night
and wake to find our ceiling glimmering,
the day a psaltery of light.

So we're out over the snow fields
before it's all seen off with a salt-lick
of Atlantic air, then home at dusk, snow-blind
from following chains of fox and crow and hare,
to a fire, a roasting bird, a ringing phone,
and voices wondering where we are.

A day foretold by images
of glassy pond, peasant and snowy roof
over the holy child iconed in gold.
Or women shawled against the goosedown air
pleading with soldiers at a shifting frontier
in the snows of television,

while in the secret dark a fresh snow falls
filling our tracks with stars.

Emlyn Williams
Hard Times

It was a bleak Christmas, and when I sniffed the frosty air, it
held no promise. For my mother, the shadow of the word she
dreaded most, 'workhouse', loomed over Mainstone Cottages;
she must have come as near despair as she can ever have been.
One night, in imitation of a band of children who had raised

piping voices at front doors and then been remunerated, I made a secret sally. Money was on my mind; having learnt 'While Shepherds Watch' in class, I set off through the drizzle in my cape, an emissary of the Tsar, and crept up to the bow-windowed houses behind the school. I would sound tremulous and proud and poor, and take a shilling home. In a dark porch, I cleared my throat, was glad Mam was not near, and started. I sounded tremulous and poor, but not proud. A light flickered through the glass, I broke off and dived into the shadows. The door opened. 'Cath oedd hi,' said Mrs Lloyd General Stores, 'it must have been a cat.' The door closed. That was Christmas 1915.

But not entirely. I took Job into the woods for holly, there was 'potas' to fill us, delicious dripping with bread drowning in it, and 'ponsh maip', mashed turnips piquantly salted; and Mam made a plum-pudding. And late on Christmas Eve, in the tiny moonlit cave of our back bedroom, I was woken by sounds such as I had never heard; as I swam up into drowsy consciousness, I thought I had died and that these deep and plangent harmonies were the first intimations of immortality. Our little family shames were washed clean; the world was still, and listening. I crept to the window, and looked up the ghostly transfigured hill. On the crest, next to the school, a choir of miners were singing carols. 'While Shepherds Watch' ... I was glad I had run away. I was facing Bethlehem Hill, and again I felt that these were the same shepherds who had sung two thousand years ago, just as it was the same moon, with its same look of impassive benediction. That was Christmas too, and anyway 1916 must be going to be better.

Leslie Norris
Maldwyn

Enoch lived in rooms above the police station, and we'd climb there, past the fire-engine on the ground floor, its brass glittering, its hoses white and spotless, past the billiard room, then up the stairs to Enoch's place. Once I saw Enoch eat. He cooked for himself a steak so huge that I could find no way to describe it to my mother. And then he covered it in fried onions. Maldwyn used to get sixpence for doing Enoch's shopping.

He had been working for Enoch on Christmas Eve. I hadn't known that. All afternoon I'd been searching for him, around the back of the garages where we had a den, in the market; I couldn't find him anywhere. Just as I thought of going home, I saw Maldwyn at the top of the street. He was singing, but when I called him he stopped and waved. The lights were coming on in the houses and shops. Some children were singing carols outside Benny Everson's door. I could have told them it was a waste of time.

'Look what Enoch gave me,' Maldwyn said. Enoch had given him ten shillings. We had never known such wealth.

'What are you going to do with it?' I asked, touching the silver with an envious finger.

'I'm going to buy Enoch a cigar,' he said, 'for Christmas. Coming over?'

We walked towards the High Street. Mr Turner, the tobacconist, was a tall, pale man, exquisitely dressed. He had a silver snuffbox and was immaculately polite to everyone who entered his shop. I knew that he and Maldwyn would be hours choosing a cigar for Enoch, I could already hear Mr Turner asking Maldwyn's opinion.

'Perhaps something Cuban?' Mr Turner would say. 'No? Something a little smaller, perhaps, a little milder?'

'Ugh?' Maldwyn would say, smiling, not understanding any of it, enjoying it all.

I couldn't stand it. When we got to the Market I told Maldwyn that I'd wait for him there. I told him I'd wait outside Marlow's where I could look at the brilliant windows of the sporting world, the rows of fishing rods and the racks of guns, the beautiful feathery hooks of salmon-flies in their perspex boxes, the soccer balls, the marvellous boxing shorts, glittering and coloured like the peacock, the blood-red boxing gloves.

Each week I spent hours at these windows and I was a long time there on Christmas Eve. Maldwyn didn't come back. At last I went home. My mother was crying and everybody in our house was quiet. Then they told me that Maldwyn was dead. He had rushed out of Mr Turner's shop, carrying in his hand two cigars in a paper bag, and run straight under a truck.

'I've been watching for him,' I said. 'Outside Marlow's. He went to buy a cigar for Enoch.'

I went to bed early and slept well. It didn't feel as if Maldwyn was dead. I thought of him as if he were in his house a few doors down the street, but when I walked past on Christmas morning the blinds were drawn across all the Farraday's windows and in some of the other houses too. The whole street was silent. And all that day I was lost, alone. We didn't enjoy Christmas in our house.

Paul Henry
Inside the MIND shop

The fake snow-spray's giant kiss
in the mirror's *Merry Xmas*
marks the spot that wills to fit
the giant into the midget.

A finger skates on the counter's pane
where a baby's boot waits to be claimed,
where Ritchie, phone tucked under his chin,
might be playing the violin
or conducting *Silent Night*,

where records, shoes, books and ties
are memorials to the Seventies,
where there's time to contemplate
the third world stuff — rugs, cushions,
a carved bird, skull caps ...

A club-foot kicks a box of cups.
Mary glances out from her wig,
hugs her faded *Woman's Own*
with its haloed baby on the front.
Something of everyone is wanted.

The dead on rails drip at the cuffs
with tags, beyond bar-codes
absorb the rain brought in,
a charmed sprig of incense.

A mitten picks up a snow dome
and shakes another storm
for the figurine children on their farm
who've seen it all before.

The door's cowbell does not distract
the one surviving browser.
He stares himself out in the mirror,
clears his throat and, suitcase in tow,
tries another *Ho! Ho! Ho!*

Richard Burton
Radicalism on Christmas Eve

I went out into the night with Dan and the other men.

Why were they sending me out at this time of night on Christmas Eve?

My mother had died when I was two years old, and I had lived with my sister and her husband ever since. I had had lots of Christmases since my mother's death, and they could already be relied on, they had always been the same. There was the growing excitement of Uncle Ben's Christmas Club (you paid a sixpence or shilling a week throughout the year), and the choosing from the catalogue — *Littlewood's Catalogue*. There was the breathless guessing at what Santa Claus would bring. What was in those anonymous brown paper parcels on top of the wardrobe? Would it be a farm with pigs in a sty, and ducks on a metal pond, and five-barred gates, and metal trees, and Kentucky fences, and a horse or two, and several cows, and a tiny bucket and a milk-maid, and a farmhouse complete with red-faced farmer and wife in the window? And a chimney on top? Pray God it wasn't Tommy Elliot's farm, which I'd played with for two years and which I feared — from glances and whispers that I'd caught between my sister and Mrs Elliot — was going to be cleaned up and bought for me for Christmas. It would be shameful to have a secondhand present. Everybody would know. It must be, if a farm at all, a spanking-new one, gleaming with fresh paint, with not a sign of the leaden base showing through.

And I would spend an hour singing Christmas carol duets from door to door with my friend Trevor, picking up a penny here and a ha'penny there. And then home at nine o'clock, perhaps to gossip with my sister and eat more nuts, and be sent to bed sleepless and agog. And now, at the time of getting to bed, I was being sent out into the night with Mad Dan and his audience — all of them with Christmas colds, and all of them drinking medicine out of little bottles kept in their inside pockets.

We went to the meeting ground of our part of the village. It was called 'The End'. It was a vacant stretch of stony ground between two rows of cottages — Inkerman and Balaclava. Both the Inkerman people and the Balaclava people called it 'The End'. Insularity, I realize now, streetophobia — to each street it was 'The End'. It should have been called 'The Middle'.

The miners had built a bonfire and stood around it, burning on one side and frozen on the other. Chestnuts and — because there had been plenty of work that year — potatoes were roasted to blackness, and eaten sprinkled with salt, smoky and steaming straight from the fire. And Mad Dan, making great gestures against the flames, told the half-listening, silent, munching miners of the lies we had been told for thousands of years, the mellifluous advice we had been told to take.

'Turn the other cheek. Turn the other cheek, boys, and get your bloody brain broken. Suffer all my children. This side of the river is torment and torture and starvation, and don't forget the sycophancy to the carriaged and horsed, the Daimlered, the bare-shouldered, remote beauties in many mansions, gleaming with the gold we made for them. Suffer all my baby-men, beat out, with great coal-hands, the black melancholy of the hymns. When you die and cross that stormy river, that roaring Jordan, there will be unimaginable delights, and God shall wipe away all tears, and there will be no more pain. Lies! Lies! Lies!'

Edith Courtney
A Visit to Kilvey Hill

We used the big rose-decorated bowl that usually held the matching jug on Mum and Dad's washing stand; and the kitchen table got strewn with empty bags, egg shells and cutlery, while the place became filled with the heady aroma of spices and stout.

Father came home noisily, banging on the front door and yelling, 'Ta-rara boom de ay, soon be Christmas Day ...' and Mother called, 'You're just in time to stir the pudding.'

He kissed her quickly, then took off his coat, whistling so his cheeks popped in and out; then we had to stir, with our eyes closed, and wish.

Me first! I gripped the wooden spoon and jabbed it in. The mixture was too stiff. I couldn't stir. I wouldn't be able to wish!

'Just stir a little bit on top. A little bit ...'

The spoon flicked, a lump of the mixture hit the ceiling and we watched in silence as it slowly unstuck itself and fell, plop, before Father's feet. We laughed and squealed, and Mother hurried because the water in the big copper in the scullery corner was boiling, the fire beneath it spluttering scarlet and orange through the edges of the black iron door.

The pudding basins were filled, the silver threepenny pieces washed and poked into the mixture, then Mother covered the basins with floured cloths, each held in place by Father while

Mother tied the string around, the greaseproof paper under the cloths crinkling and creasing excitingly. Mother tied the knots very tightly, knot over knot and knotting again, then with brisk short steps she carried them out, pushing a long stick through the top knots of the cloths so her hand was well away from the bubbling heat of the water and, amid the steam, she slowly lowered the basins in, arranging them so they each got their fair share of boiling water and room.

Then she cleared the table, and quickly I was dressed in outdoor clothing, Mother smothering my face in cold cream because of the wind. Father took off his collar and tie and sighed into his deep armchair. His canvassing for the day was over, now it was time for Mother and me to go collecting. We went out and the wind cut us pink.

We went down, but turned off, towards the mountain, and I clutched Mother's hand in delight. We were on the other side of the shunting yards, and now we were on the bank of the canal, and there, on the rust and silver water, just against the steps, bobbed a little boat.

The lean, leather-skinned man seemed elderly, and saw us coming. He stood up, his hands clutching the stonework beyond our feet, the boat swaying under him. He called, and the wind whipped his voice away. Mother held her full dark skirts about her with one hand and me with the other as we went down the slippery steps.

'You never bin on a ferry afore?' the man said to me, and he didn't have a coat, just a striped flannel shirt with the sleeves rolled up, and his arms were brown and alive with muscle. I shook my head and the boat swayed and dipped as Mother sat. I went carefully beside her, facing the man, and to my delighted horror he began to row. The boat left the wall!

Water bubbled gently near my feet. 'I must get a plank across there,' the man said, and his neck went taut as he pulled the boat on.

From water and the opposite bank my fascinated gaze rose to the stark, hoar-frost-covered, Kilvey Hill before us. All its aspirations to greenery murdered by the works at its feet; copper, spelter, tin, all spouting smoke that was laden with fumes and chemical debris. Pollution as it is never seen today. To me then, and to me today, Kilvey Hill is beautiful. Tricks of the weather bring it closer or move it further away, but that Christmas, just after my seventh birthday, Kilvey Hill exuded dominance, power, and I was suitably awed.

Dewi Roberts
The Invitation

Christmas was fast approaching and the normally restrained atmosphere in the office of *Sommersby, Renshaw and Davies, Solicitors*, became more relaxed and from time to time, the occasional unexpected joke would be shared by the normally reticent Mr Renshaw and the clerk Tommy Jones. Tommy was twenty-eight, easy-going and evidently something of a ladies' man. This side of his character was of particular interest to Mrs Hesketh-Williams, the blowzy, middle-aged receptionist, who had a keen ear for any whiff of gossip.

Peter Lewis was the junior, seventeen, not long out of school and very anxious to create the right impression. In some ways he regarded Tommy as, if not a rôle model, at least as someone he could emulate in certain ways. Tommy, after all, wasn't troubled by self-doubt and a nagging self-consciousness, and then there was his seemingly easy ability to attract women ....

So when Mr Sommersby handed out cards to all his staff inviting them to a Christmas Eve party at his home, Peter regarded the invitation with a mixture of pleasure and apprehension. After all, it wasn't the kind of party to which he, an office dogsbody and the son of a coalman, was normally invited. Would he find himself out of his depth? Could he get through the evening without making a blunder? If he did not go to the party he would only spend the evening brooding and wondering what he might be missing, and this forced his decision.

After arriving home from work on Christmas Eve, he began

to prepare for the evening ahead. In the bathroom of his parents' small terraced house he had a bath, shaved for the second time that day, and rubbed a generous handful of Brylcreem into his hair, before combing it very carefully. He then went through to his bedroom and put on his only suit, blue and double-breasted. As he gazed at himself in a full-length mirror this did nothing to raise his confidence. He then went downstairs, said goodbye to his parents, and stepped out into the frosty night. As he climbed the Bwlch, and the lights of the town receded behind him, he felt as though he was taking a journey into the unknown.

He plodded on until he came to the driveway leading to the Sommersby's large Georgian house. As he walked towards the open front door, he could hear voices and laughter from within. He stepped inside and found himself in a very large hall with a roaring log-fire and a splendidly-decorated large Christmas tree. About twenty people stood around with glasses in their hands. Mr Sommersby came through jauntily from an adjoining room and spotted him. He was a dapper, grey-haired man in his early fifties.

'Welcome, Peter,' he said with a broad smile. 'Happy Christmas. Let me get you a drink.'

Peter accepted a beer, and Mr Sommersby was joined by a woman with shoulder-length auburn hair and striking blue eyes, who was dressed in a fine blue satin dress. Peter thought her incredibly beautiful and her sudden presence took his breath away. He thought her more lovely than many of the actresses whom he saw in the films which he regularly watched in the Odeon at Colwyn Bay.

'Lydia — this is Peter. You've heard me mentioning him many times. Peter, this is my wife.'

They shook hands, and Mr Sommersby turned to chat to another guest.

'It's good to meet the men behind the scenes in the office,' Lydia Sommersby said. 'It's surprising that we haven't met before now really.'

There was a pause and Peter nervously took a sip from his glass.

'Christmas is such a wonderful time of the year,' she continued. 'I mean it brings out the best in everyone. Don't you agree?'

'Oh, yes I do,' responded Peter with an ever-increasing sense of nervousness.

By this time, more guests were arriving and Lydia Sommersby excused herself and hurried off to greet them, leaving Peter isolated from the surrounding groups who were chatting way, sometimes laughing loudly at a joke or observation. For what seemed an eternity, Peter stood watching them until Selwyn Higgins came up behind him and began asking him about work in the office. Higgins was a local butcher and chairman of the finance committee of the local council. It was not long before he was boasting about his administrative expertise. Peter pretended to be interested, but was unable to disguise an expression of utter boredom. But, suddenly, over Higgins' right shoulder, Peter became aware of Lydia Sommersby again, beckoning to him from across the room. Excitedly he left Higgins in full flow and hurried off.

'I could see you were cornered there by that windbag,' she laughed. 'Would you mind just giving me a hand in the kitchen for a moment?' She led him down a long passageway into a large, very warm, kitchen. Placing a tray on the table, she turned suddenly and faced him.

'Let's have a moment's rest from the others,' she said smiling.

He wondered why this stunning woman should wish to spend any time with him, especially at Christmas.

'Peter, do you mind if I say something? She took him by his clammy right hand. 'You're ill at ease, aren't you? You're very shy and you lack confidence.' She gave his hand a squeeze. 'But I want to tell you that there's absolutely no reason why you should feel like that.'

Peter's temples were pounding by this time and the entire situation seemed unreal.

'I don't know what to say,' he spluttered.

'Then don't say anything.' She stood very close. 'If I were to make a wish right now,' she said softly. 'It would be that you might kiss me.'

He moved to plant a kiss on her cheek, but she turned and pressed her body against him and gently brushed her lips against his. But the kiss then developed into something more searching as she began to explore his mouth with her tongue. Suddenly, Peter felt a sharp spasm of desire and his hands moved slowly to her breasts. As he caressed them gently, kissing her on her neck as he did so, the thought of what he was doing, and the fear of them being discovered, made him suddenly and clumsily end their embrace.

'That was lovely,' she said with a gentle smile. 'So don't ever let me see you looking like one of life's rejects again. When you came here tonight I don't suppose you expected to be seduced by the boss's wife!'

'This is a Christmas I'll always remember,' he replied.

'Well, you must come again next Christmas and, who knows, you may have more of the same.' She gave him a peck on his cheek. 'And now we must get back to the others.'

At the end of the evening, as he walked back down the hill to the town, Peter was giddy with exhilaration, and wanted to tell the whole world what had happened. How Tommy Jones would envy him! And Mrs Hesketh-Williams would certainly make a meal of it. He smiled to himself and felt a warm glow.

Suddenly he raised his voice in song and *Oh Come All Ye Faithful* broke the silence of the night. As he stopped at a field gate, he gazed up at the stars, as though for the first time, and noticed how very bright and clear they were.

Meic Stephens
Dymuniad y Tymor

Tonight, switching on the television news,
I heard that the poet Gwenallt Jones was dead;
it's Christmas eve, my daughters are in bed
wrapped by the snows of Tir na n-Og. Now's

the moment when, like fathers everywhere,
I must play Siôn Corn. What shall I wish for
them? Not the old, jingling compliments, nor
the new, tinsel plenty that is our share —

I would not spoil a little child's delight
but these are purchased at the cheapest stall.
No, because that man and poet died tonight

I have only one wish: may they belong
to Wales as he did, cherishing most of all
his faith, his language and his living song.

Ronnie Knox Mawer
Gifts from the Chemist's Shop

One evening I remember the Worshipful Master of the Brom-
field Lodge called to wish the compliments of the season.
Father had just taken late postal delivery of a brown paper
parcel.

'Somebody's sent you a pretty big Christmas parcel,'
quipped the Worshipful Master. Father laughed grimly as he
snipped the the string and brought out a number of dingy grey
woollen garments.

'Care for an army bed-jacket, W.M.?' the astonished visitor
was asked. Father had written for another bargain advertised
in the *Daily Mail*.

'Finest wool. Surplus to military requirements, 7/6d the
dozen, minimum order.' We four children were already wearing
ours.

Apart from Army surplus clothing most of the cupboard
space at 'Resthaven' seemed to be taken up with Father's
boots. He only seemed to use the one pair which my second
sister and I had to clean — an uneasy task because Father had
very hot feet. We were strangely slow to associate those lace-up

boots with the ones worn by Santa Claus. We should have guessed. Our Christmas stockings invariably contained nail brushes, combs and sticking plaster, all from Father's shop, as well as the coal tar soap and a strange board game known as *Gibbs Giant Decay*. It was played with counters marked *Gibbs Toothcare* which were sent back to START AGAIN whenever a landing was made in the dungeon of Giant Decay!

Kate Roberts
Buying the Cards

Many people down from the country today; crowded around the Christmas cards. 'Will you choose one with a nice verse on it?' said one after the other. Lloyd crammed into the shop as far as he could. 'Hi, Lloyd, give these people your literary advice.' And he pushed through them to the counter. Selling chocolate at the other end I heard, 'There you are, quite a good one with a picture of Mary and Joseph. Here's one with a pretty little dog on it.' 'I have enough dogs at home.' 'A cat then?' 'No, a picture of a little house sheltering in a grove of trees in the middle of the snow, with a red robin at the door.' 'Here it is, the very thing, with holly as a bonus.' 'They're much too dear at sixpence.' 'So is your milk,' from Lloyd. 'Nobody uses milk to make Christmas cards.' 'You never know; people are very clever today.' The shop full of laughter. 'There's a pretty one, Miss Humphreys, a picture of two sweethearts kissing.' I didn't have to turn round to see if Miss Humphreys was blushing.

translated by Joseph P. Clancy

A.J. Cronin
Grateful Patients

With the approach of Christmas the weather turned colder — crisp frosty days and still, starry nights. The iron hard roads rang under Andrew's feet. The clear air was like an exhilarating wine. Already shaping in his mind was the next step which he would take in his great assault on the problem of dust inhalation. His findings amongst his own patients had raised his hopes high, and now he had obtained permission from Vaughan to extend the field of his investigation by making a systematic examination of all the workers in the three anthracite sinkings — a marvellous opportunity. He planned to use the pit workers and surfacemen as controls. He would begin at the start of the New Year.

On Christmas Eve he returned from surgery to Vale View with an extraordinary sense of spiritual anticipation and physical well-being. As he walked up the road it was impossible to escape the signs of the impending festival. The miners made much of Christmas here. For the past week the front room in each house had been locked against the children, festooned with paper streamers, toys hidden in the drawers of the chest and a steady accumulation of good things to eat, cake, oranges, sweet sugar biscuits, all bought with the club money paid out at this time of year, laid upon the table.

Christine had made her own decorations of holly and mistletoe in gay expectation. But to-night as he came into the house he saw at once an extra excitement upon her face.

'Don't say a word,' she said quickly holding out her hand. 'Not a single word! Just shut your eyes and come with me!'

He allowed her to lead him into the kitchen. There, on the table lay a number of parcels, clumsily made up, some merely wrapped in newspaper, but each with a little note attached. In a flash he realised that they were presents from his patients. Some of the gifts were not wrapped up at all.

'Look, Andrew!' Christine cried. 'A goose! And two ducks! And a lovely iced cake! And a bottle of elderberry wine! Isn't it kind of them! Isn't wonderful they should want to give them to you.'

He simply could not speak. It overwhelmed him, this kindly evidence that the people of his district had at last begun to appreciate, to like him. With Christine at his shoulder he read the notes, the handwriting laboured and illiterate, some scrawled in pencil upon old envelopes turned inside out. 'Your grateful patient at 3 Cefan Row.' 'With thanks from Mrs Williams.' One lopsided gem from Sam Bevan, 'Thanks for gettin' me out for Christmas, doctor *bach*' — so they went on.

Irene Thomas
Christmas Goose

Downstairs,
I had heard of the Gander
and the violence.

I watched
the annual pantomime of goose feathers
the hissing and the cackling.

My Grandmother, knee deep in down,
plucked the Christmas goose.
Feathers flew from her fingers
and cushioned the wooden chairs,
settled a white cover on the table.
I clapped my hands
and the feathers danced to set patterns
over the oiled cloth,
a ballet along familiar lines.
They hung in the air
and with a sharp intake,
filled my mouth until I spat out.
I stuffed armfuls into bolsters
and pillows cased in ticking.
Up to my elbows in warm snow,
I chilled.

The pimples
and the comic appearance of the stripped bird
gave rise to old chestnuts,
'His goose is cooked',
drew ribald laughter-come-to-crying.

Upstairs
on chesty nights,
I slipped into goose-greased dreams
held between the bony knees of nightmare.
White winged sheets
beat like angels guarding
as my grandfather played his part
with the cutting edge,
and circled the long white neck
of Mother Goose
with a gash of ruby.
I buried my face in the pillow
to deaden the screaming and the song,
but feathers suffocated.

Leslie Norris
Great, Invisible Birds

'I had a cousin in Cardiganshire who was an expert with geese,'
my uncle said after a silence. 'Kept all the varieties in his time.
People used to come from all over the country to buy breeding
stock from him. Oh, what a sight to see his flocks on the moors
— great flocks of geese, marching like Prussians! He used to
clip their wings at the elbow so they couldn't fly, and then,
once they were old enough, out they'd go on the open moors,
white geese, grey geese. They never strayed. At dusk they'd
come high-stepping into his yard and the whole mountain
would be full of their voices. I often stayed with him when I
was young.

'He sent us a goose every year — two geese: one for Michaelmas and another for Christmas, always trussed and ready for cooking. He used to send them by bus — a bewildering journey, with many changes — but none of them ever failed to reach us. I used to wait here, on the square, for the bus to come in from Brecon toward late afternoon. The conductor would hand me a large hamper with our goose inside, and I'd stagger home with it. We used to cook it on a spit, rotating it in front of a blaze of a fire, a pan beneath to catch the melting fat. We took turns at basting it as it spun slowly — first one way, then the other — so that it wouldn't burn. Every Michaelmas and every Christmas for years. What feasts we had then! Nor was that the end of the goose's usefulness. After the cooking we put the solidified goose grease in jars and kept it as a cure for sore throats and chest colds and bronchitis. I can remember my mother rubbing it on my bare chest and throat when I was a small boy. I can remember its gross smell, the thick feel of the grease on my skin. I hated that, although the old people swore by it as a curative.

'And even the bed I slept on owed its comfort to my cousin's geese, for the bed was stuffed with feathers from his birds. My mother made a huge envelope of blue and white striped ticking and filled it with goose feathers, making the whole thing plump and soft as a cloud. We all sleep well when we're young, but nobody could have slept softer and deeper than I did in my goose-feather bed.'

My uncle held out his hand in front of him. 'You see this hand?' he asked. 'The hand is a superb instrument. This hand of mine can do all manner of things: it can wield a hammer, pick up a pin, it can point a chisel to the exact splitting place of a stone, it can create, it can destroy. My cousin's hands were to do with geese. He had huge hands. Here, on the inside of his thumb and forefinger, he had long callouses, incredibly hard, from feathering geese. Every week he would kill and pluck some of his birds for market, and many more near Christmas and other busy times. He had slaughtered thousands over the years. And when he plucked them he did it swiftly, expertly, and the soft flesh would not be bruised or torn when he finished. I've seen him kill and dress hundreds of birds. He was an artist.'

'How old was he, Wynford?' Mr Carrington asked.

'Not a lot older than I,' said my uncle. 'Seven or eight years. But that's a lot when you're young. He was already at work on the farm when I was a young boy visiting there.'

'What's he doing now?' asked Selby Davis.

'He's dead,' my uncle said softly. 'Yes, he's dead these many years.' He shifted on his painted stool. He was far away, visiting an old sadness. 'He's been dead for years,' he repeated. 'One Christmas he had many geese, and he set to work early, day after day, killing and preparing them. The weather was intolerably cold. The mountains had a fall of snow, two feet deep and deeper in drifts. It never stopped freezing. Night and day not a gust of wind — only the deep stillness of frost. My cousin kept the dead birds in a long barn, where they hung in rows, head down. The bitter cold worried my cousin. It was bringing in the wild things off the hills, the rats and foxes. He found himself staying more and more near his filling barn.

'One night he awoke from sleep, bright awake at once, certain that something was wrong. It was just after three in the morning. He hurried into his thick clothes and wrapped a blanket over his shoulders. There wasn't a sound in the yard; even the living birds were silent. The brilliant snow threw back every gleam of light, redoubled it, so the night was unnaturally lit. The barn door was locked and safe. Nothing was out of place. He opened the door and went in. The dead geese hung in their rows before him, untouched, pallid. The night was pitilessly still. My cousin moved along the stiff files, alert, waiting for something to happen.

'Then, in the cold barn, as if from high above him, he heard the call of geese, far away, the crying of wild geese out of the empty sky. He could hear them clearly, although he knew they were not there. He did not move. In an instant the barn was full of their loud honking; their flailing wings beat under the sturdy roof. He closed his eyes in terror, he wrapped his arms about his bent head, and through his barn flew the heavy skeins of great, invisible birds. Their crying filled his ears; the still air was buffeted by their plunging flight, on and on, until the last bodiless goose was flown and the long, wild voices were gone. He stood in the cold of his barn and opened his eyes. What he saw was this: he saw the hanging corpses of his own geese, every one swaying, every one swinging gently. And that was the most frightening of all.'

My uncle sighed. 'Poor old boy,' he said. 'Poor old lad. After a while they took him to Swansea, to the mental hospital, and he died there.'

'How do you know this?' asked Ginty Willis.

'He told me,' said Uncle Wynford. 'I went down to see him, and he told me. He was a young man, only thirty-two when he died. He had killed thousands of geese, thousands of them.'

'What was his name, Uncle?' I asked. I stood in the warm day as cold as if I were in the heart of that long-dead winter and were standing under the roof among the swaying corpses of Christmas geese.

'Good God!' my uncle said. 'Are you still here? Get to school, get to school! You'll be late.' I turned and ran.

All day my friends were indolent in the heat of the quiet classroom, moving sleepily through their work, but all I could see were the high arrows of the streaming geese, all I could hear was their faint and melancholy crying, and the imagined winter was all about me.

Idris Davies
Christmas Eve 1946

The shepherds watch tonight again
The star above the byre
Where Mary's child is born again
Unto the heart's desire.

The angels sing tonight again
  Of God who gives to earth
His gift of love and joy again
  To all who seek his mirth.

The wise men walk tonight again
  To Bethlehem afar
To worship and to praise again
  The babe beneath the star.

And we shall sing tonight again
  The songs of other years,
Until our hearts are young again
  Behind our hidden tears.

Ruth Bidgood
Solstice

December moon swells:
Virgo rises in the east.
Behind early curtains we hide
from gentle exacting light
in controllable brightness,
and tame to tinsel patterns
the immortality-tree.
We are as adamantly shut,
as helpless, as the solstice-door,
that will not escape
the imminent shattering of locks
at the push of a child's hand.

Gladys Mary Coles
Touching Balloons, Llandudno

I'd hoped for the reprieve of rain
to save me from the all-week-dreaded party.
I'd prayed for a tide-borne storm
to beat across the bay, break on the West Shore
jewelling our Christmas windows.
But the rain dwindled, clouds split back,
citrus sunlight drenched the Conwy headland.
We struggled along the rinsed promenade
where the White Rabbit raised a paw
saluting me in sympathy. Again I scanned
the Great Orme's cliffs, grey mass merged with sky,
to glimpse the eyrie where we'd clung
last summer — my mother, Auntie and I —
mist-beguiled on sheep-tracks slippery as ice,
drawn to the gull-crested edge above the sea.
That giddying wait on the precipice,
that swinging-out, roped, in a rescuer's arms.

Ahead, the Christmas lights of Mostyn Street
red, green, silver, tossing in the wind;
a snatch of carol singing near the giant fir.
For primary schools, the Town Hall treat —
in its bright chasm I stood unsure
my mother repeating she'd return at three.
Joining the rows of children as they clapped
two tumbling clowns, I feared their dripping eyes,
noses like raw meat, their monstrous mouths.

Above us swayed the balloons,
bright clusters suspended from the ceiling —
red globes, blue spheres, yellow planets.
Who will be chosen to touch the balloons?
Silenced by teachers, we gathered underneath,
our names inside a shaken biscuit tin
selected by Father Christmas, tall as a pine.

My tiny *no* was trapped inside my throat
as he lifted me to a dizzying height.
I saw below the gulfing waves, sheer crags
where a bird-nesting boy had fallen.
And yet, cheered on, I reached for the balloons,
pulled at a dangling string. The clusters broke away,
coloured moons filling the room, floating
into the children's waiting hands.
I saw the seagulls soaring to their ledges,
and a Celtic cross shining on the sea.

Selyf Roberts
A Wartime Exile

During the last war Selyf Roberts was captured by
the Italians and interned. When he became ill he
spent a recovery period in a university hospital in
Parma.

I lay back in the clean, white bed. It was the night before
Christmas. It had grown late before any of us was asleep, and
although everyone was quiet I could sense that some of the
others were of restless mind, without knowing why. Expec-
tantly awake, perhaps, because there had been talk going the
rounds that next day there were to be Christmas parcels from
the Red Cross. The evening hours slid into night, and I
watched the stars move from pane to pane across the tall
windows along one side of the ward. There had been a fall of
snow the previous day and all that morning, but by now the
leaden clouds had dispersed and the clear dark-blue firmament
formed a fitting back-cloth to the silver and gold of the
constellations. And as the clouds were driven away, the frost
came — frost and stars, and the night. And Christmas Eve.

I was nowhere near sleep when the bells began. They pierced
the air without any warning, and for a while nothing could be

heard save the careless confusion of their sound: the sound of bells from churches and convents and schools and colleges, all tumbling together like a cascade over the frost. But in a moment I was able to put an order to things and my hearing became a listening, so that the various bells were greeting me and I could distinguish one from another. I could hear the playful tunes of the church just up the street, and the more priestly boom of the Cathedral yonder; one bell was ringing out a single tenor note, as though it had escaped for the night from the accursed company of book and candle, and with its cheerful tinkling was interwoven with alto and contralto of other bells pealing in rhythmic dignity. A round of six was competing with another of eight, and yet another octave interfered temporarily to put them out of my hearing with a tumult of notes which seemed to be sent forth any old how. But the night ensured that the breeze would, every now and then, disseminate the bishop's sonorous bell, keeping discipline and preventing the rejoicing from becoming a carnival.

There was no war in the bells' world; there was no dispute among men to prevent the dawn of Christmas. There was no discord among those who listened to the anthem of gold, frankincense and myrrh. Had they been listening, the bells of Parma would have been pealing in the ears of Hitler and Mussolini and Churchill and Stalin, just as they rang out for me. For a few minutes I felt the situation to be too much for me. I couldn't understand how it was that the years had so injected poison into the veins of mankind as to allow the sound of gunfire to mingle with the ringing of bells. My leaping mind turned to my home in Wales, and I failed to understand what complexity of life it was that bade the bells of Parma ring so gleefully while the tongues of the bells at Llandrillo-yn-Rhos had been tied and were mute.

translated by Meic Stephens

Richard Hughes
Bedtime Anticipation

Well, you may maintain, when we were children Christmas
was Christmas, all stockings and stomach-aches ... But was it,
always, even then? When I think of the Christmas of my
childhood, there is one single memory standing out vividly
among the rest.

For three days I had been in bed with earache, and it showed
no signs of mending. But violent pain, if it lasts long enough,
seems somehow to defeat itself. I had long since stopped
crying. The pain seemed to have translated itself into a sort of
grumbling roar, like the sea, above which my mind hovered
birdlike and unnaturally excited. Sleep, that Christmas Eve,
was impossible — and when I was warned that if I could not
get to sleep Father Christmas would never come, it only served
to distress me. To avoid the disaster, I thought, I would at least
feign sleep. And then — ecstatic thought! — by peering
through half-shut lids I might even catch a mortal glimpse of
him.

So, for what seemed hours I lay with eyes shut, motionless,
listening to the growling of my pain. At last the door opened
and someone tiptoed to the foot of my bed .... When I saw who
it was, the disappointment and disillusion, that would have
been violent enough at any time, were overpowering. My poor
excited mind, struck in the middle of its hovering, began to fall
... down, down, in an ever increasing spiral like the death dive
of a stricken aeroplane; down, down until suddenly, almost
before the orange had been well and truly rammed into the toe
of the stocking, catastrophe accomplished what nothing given
in a bottle by a doctor or sung by mother could accomplish,
and it landed in a deep comfortable, and dreamless sleep.

Joseph P. Clancy
A Cywydd for Christmas

Each year a bit more weary
As we complete our home-made
Liturgy: the last-minute
Cleaning up, the candle lit,
The tree (defiantly real)
Trimmed, and the tiny figures
Set carefully in the crèche,
The final Advent service
Interrupting the hurried
Wrapping of gifts in each room
(Glorious waste of gay paper),
And the children's presents fetched
From closets in their absence —
Whether in bed or at church —
And strewn through the living room
For morning's still exciting
Entry and flurried finding,
Though boy and girl to become
Man and woman must challenge
Our rite, and we watch it change
Slowly, inexorably.

Accept, dear, alteration
In them and in us, affirm
The bond of love unbroken
In spite of all departures
From childhood, custom, and home,
As we celebrate once more
Our ritual's consummation.
This has not changed: the quiet
Exchange of gifts, and the kiss,
Without passion, confirming
Each year the new birth of Love.

Christmas Day

Rowland Watkyns
Upon Christ's Nativity or Christmas

From three dark places Christ came forth this day:
First from his Father's bosom, where he lay
Concealed till now, then from the typic Law,
Where we his manhood but by figure saw;
And lastly from his Mother's womb he came
To us a perfect God and perfect man.
Now in a Manger lies the eternal Word,
The Word he is, yet can no speech afford.
He is the Bread of Life, yet hungry lies,
The living Fountain, yet for drink he cries.
He cannot help or clothe himself at need,
Who did the lilies clothe and ravens feed.
He is the Light of Lights, yet now doth shroud
His glory with our nature as a cloud;
He came to us a little one, that we
Like little children might in malice be;
Little he is, and wrapped in clouts, lest he
Might strike us dead if clothed with majesty.
Christ had four beds, and those not soft, nor brave,
The Virgin's Womb, the Manger, Cross, and Grave.
The Angels sung this day, and so will I,
That have more reason to be glad, than they.

Francis Kilvert
An Icy Bath

Sunday, Christmas Day 1870

As I lay praying in the early morning I thought I heard a sound
of distant bells. It was an intense frost. I sat down in my bath
upon a sheet of thick ice which broke in the middle into large
pieces whilst the sharp points and jagged edges stuck all round

the side of the tub like *chevaux de frise*, not particularly comfortable to the naked thighs and loins because the keen ice cut like broken glass. The ice water stung and scorched like fire. I had to collect the floating pieces of ice and pile them on a chair before I could use the sponge and then I had to thaw the sponge in my hands for it was a mass of ice. The morning was most brilliant. Walked to the Sunday school with Gibbins and the road sparkled with millions of rainbows, the seven colours gleaming in every glittering point of hoar-frost. The Church was very cold in spite of two roaring fires.

Eiluned Lewis
A Victorian Festive Service

On Christmas Day the Peters family attended matins in the Cathedral, since no service was held on that day in any of the nonconformist chapels of St Idris. Leaving the house, in which a fine flavour of goose was already apparent, they trooped through the Cross, exchanging greetings with their neighbours, and holding fast to their hats and bonnets because of the boisterous wind that came galloping to meet them across the bare land and over the slate and whitewashed roofs that tumble down the hill to the Cathedral Close. Beyond the tall spire of the Methodist Tabernacle they could see the white waves whipping the tail of the Bishop Rock, and when they reached the gateway of the city wall the wind was so strong that Mamma's skirts blew out like a ship's canvas, and Philip's little velvet cap went bowling down the Thirty-Nine Articles, which is the name given to the grey flight of steps that go down to the Cathedral.

But below in the Close there was shelter from the tearing wind, and as always the comfortable sound of rooks in the bare sycamores. They met more people here, all hurrying in to sing and pray: the big family of boys from the Vicarage, the Dean's sister who kept house for him, the two red-haired daughters of the Archdeacon and the young lady engaged to marry the Vicar Choral.

Everyone looked cheerful and Matty thought they had all decked themselves in their prettiest clothes. The Dean's sister wore her sealskin jacket, and the wife of the Minor Canon had bunches of red berries and glossy leaves on her bonnet. Yet no one, Matty was sure, looked as pretty as Mamma in her grey mantle with the chinchilla fur round her throat.

But it was remarkable how little those things counted once they had entered the Cathedral, and how small and unimportant everyone appeared under the great arches.

> *O come, all ye faithful,*
> *Joyful and triumphant!*

sang the choir, and their voices made still more arches of sound. Down through the ages the sweet, shrill voices of boys, those short-lived yet deathless voices, had invited the faithful people to come to Bethlehem; and now once again it was Christmas morning.

Catherine Fisher
Nativity

Out of the hedges sheep turn from the wind.
Lanes are empty over the bitter hills.
Nobody travels for nobody knows the way;
today everyone will be counted where they are.
The people have hidden themselves; they've gone to ground
deep in the warm rooms and the charity halls,
burrowing into the red heart of the day,
the comfort of stories, the bright unanswerable star.
But the heart is beating, suddenly beating
subtle and soft so the sheep look up and listen;
beating in the scarlet rotting berries;

in the tangle of the wind among the trees;
in the barn where the drunken tramp is singing;
in the corner of the church where the candle slowly stiffens.

R.S. Thomas
Christmas

There is a morning:
Time brings it nearer,
Brittle with frost
And starlight. The owls sing
In the parishes. The people rise
And walk to the churches'
Stone lanterns, there to kneel
And eat the new bread
Of love, washing it down
With the sharp taste
Of blood they will shed.

Thomas Love Peacock
A Festive Gathering At Headlong Hall

The ivied towers of Caernarvon, the romantic woods of Tan-y-bwlch, the heathy hills of Kernioggau, the sandy shores of Tremadoc, the mountain recesses of Bedd-Gelert, and the lonely lakes of Capel-Cerig, re-echoed to the voices of the delighted ostlers and postilions, who reaped on this happy day their wintry harvest. Landlords and landladies, waiters, chambermaids, and toll-gate keepers, roused themselves from the torpidity which the last solitary tourist, flying with the yellow leaves on the wings of the autumnal wind, had left them to enjoy till the returning spring ....

It was the custom for the guests to assemble at dinner on the day of the ball, and depart on the following morning after breakfast. Sleep during this interval was out of the question.

The ball-room was adorned with great taste and elegance, under the direction of Miss Caprioletta and her friend Miss Cephalis, who were themselves its most beautiful ornaments; even though romantic Meirion, the pre-eminent in loveliness, sent many of its loveliest daughters to grace the festive scene. Numberless were the solicitations of the dazzled swains of Cambria for the honour of the two first dances with the one or the other of these fascinating friends; but little availed, on this occasion, the pedigree lineally traced from Caractacus or King Arthur: their two philosophical lovers, neither of whom could have given the least account of his great-great-great-grandfather, had engaged them many days before. Mr Panscope chafed and fretted like Llugwy in his bed of rocks, when the object of his adoration stood up with his rival: but he consoled himself with a lively damsel from the vale of Edeirnion, having first compelled Miss Cephalis to promise her hand for the fourth set.

The ball was accordingly opened by Miss Caprioletta and Mr Foster, which gave rise to much speculation among the Welsh gentry, as to who this Mr Foster could be; some of the more learned among them secretly resolving to investigate most profoundly the antiquity of the name of Foster, and ascertain what right a person so denominated could have to open the most illustrious of all possible balls with the lovely Caprioletta Headlong, the only sister of Harry Headlong, Esquire, of Headlong Hall, in the Vale of Llanberris, the only surviving male representative of the antediluvian family of Headlong Ap-Rhaiader.

When the two first dances were ended, Mr Escot, who did not choose to dance with anyone but his adorable Cephalis, looking round for a convenient seat, discovered Mr Jenkison in a corner by the side of the Reverend Doctor Gaster, who was keeping excellent time with his nose to the lively melody of the harp and fiddle ....

At the end of the third set, supper was announced; and the

party, pairing off like turtles, adjourned to the supper-room. The squire was now the happiest of mortal men, and the little butler the most laborious. The centre of the largest table was decorated with a model of Snowdon, surmounted with an enormous artificial leek, the leaves of angelica, and the bulb of blanc-mange. A little way from the summit was a tarn, or mountain-pool, supplied through concealed tubes with an inexhaustible flow of milk-punch, which, dashing in cascades down the miniature rocks, fell into the more capacious lake below, washing the mimic foundations of Headlong Hall. The reverend doctor handed Miss Philomela to the chair most conveniently situated for enjoying this interesting scene, protesting he had never before been sufficiently impressed with the magnificence of that mountain, which he now perceived to be well worthy of all the fame it had obtained.

Nigel Wells
Y Plygaint

In the season of Winter
The final and first
Small skin covered god
Breathed to life

In dire of the weather
Our hope into bone
We wake at his waking
To light

The faithful report
Troop to the several sites

You Cardigan ladies
On with the lace
French chalked to heighten the white

We travel by candelling
File behind fire
Pilgrim in tallow fired night

Chapel and church call their scatter
The faithful repair
Luminous choirs in a gather
Carollers lit in the rare

Oh Lord hear our seasonal singing
Our tunefully outfitted air
Our stream of particular worship
Small Lordly in snowing
Our prayer

Bells make silver of drear
Cut it to clear
Ring and rouse by their ringing
The pious to praise

Sound of them strays
Steel peelers reeling the phrase
Dinning the ear lest the sensory's veer
Iron on the brassy cast plays

The joyfully word

Our Lord under litter
In draperies curled

Love's little lad in the world

He here
The gloria gongs

Sharpened to man shape
Great God's little snip
We make our oblation in writ

We thin on the ground
Would be throng on the air
And offer such verse as we dare

In season of winter these scribble and bits
Small saviour come down and the dove

Oh Lord in the greeny
Our Lord in the pink
We offer such jots
As we have

Francis Kilvert
A Christmas Day Funeral

Wednesday. Christmas Day 1878

Very hard frost last night. At Presteign the thermometer fell to
2 degrees, showing 30 degrees of frost. At Monnington it fell
to 4. Last night is said to have been the coldest night for 100
years. The windows of the house and Church were so thick
with frost rime that we could not see out. We could not look
through the Church windows all day. Snow lay on the ground
and the day was dark and gloomy with a murky sky. A fair
morning congregation considering the weather. By Miss
Newton's special desire Dora and I went to the Cottage to eat
our Christmas dinner at 1.30 immediately after service.

Immediately after dinner I had to go back to the church for
the funeral of little Davie of the Old Weston who died on
Monday was fixed for 2.15. The weather was dreadful, the
snow driving in blinding clouds and the walking tiresome. Yet
the funeral was only 20 minutes late. The Welcome Home, as
it chimed softly and slowly to greet the little pilgrim coming to
his rest, sounded bleared and muffled through the thick snowy
air. The snow fell thickly all through the funeral service and at

the service by the grave a kind woman offered her umbrella which a kind young fellow came and held over my head. The woman and man were Mrs Richards and William Jackson. I asked the poor mourners to come in and rest and warm themselves but they would not and went into Church. The poor father, David Davies the shepherd, was crying bitterly for the loss of his little lamb. Owing to the funeral it was rather late before we began the afternoon service. There were very few people in Church beside the mourners. The afternoon was very dark. I was obliged to move close to the great south window to read the lessons and could hardly see even then. I preached from Luke ii. 7. 'There was no room for them in the inn,' and connected the little bed in the churchyard in which we had laid Davie to rest with the manger cradle at Bethlehem.

Huw Jones
Christmas Card

The blue-robed Virgin, shepherds
and kings, bordered by candles,
choir-boys, bells — a bright mosaic
of stained glass.

Through this window
a churchyard glitters with frost,
glows with the crimson fires of
glass-blowers. Workmen, in rough
leather aprons, cough and curse
above their pans of liquid
greens and golds.

A young woman
appears through the smoke, hoping
to roast a few chestnuts,
keep her baby warm.

Dylan Thomas
That Bright White Snowball of Christmas

Now out of that bright white snowball of Christmas gone comes the stocking, the stocking of stockings, that hung at the foot of the bed with the arm of a golliwog dangling over the top and small bells ringing in the toes. There was a company, gallant and scarlet but never nice to taste though I always tried when very young, of belted and busbied and musketed lead soldiers so soon to lose their heads and legs in the wars on the kitchen table after the tea-things, the mince-pies, and the cakes that I helped to make by stoning the raisins and eating them, had been cleared away; and a bag of moist and many-coloured jelly-babies and a folded flag and a false nose and a tram-conductor's cap and a machine that punched tickets and rang a bell; never a catapult; once, by a mistake that no one could explain, a little hatchet; and a rubber buffalo, or it may have been a horse, with a yellow head and haphazard legs; and a celluloid duck that made, when you pressed it, a most unduck-like noise, a mewing moo that an ambitious cat might make who wishes to be a cow; and a painting-book in which I could make the grass, the trees, the sea, and the animals any colour I pleased: and still the dazzling sky-blue sheep are grazing in the red field under a flight of rainbow-beaked and pea-green birds.

Christmas morning was always over before you could say Jack Frost. And look! suddenly the pudding was burning! Bang the gong and call the fire-brigade and the book-loving firemen! Someone found the silver threepenny-bit with a currant on it; and the someone was always Uncle Arnold. The motto in my cracker read:

Let's all have fun this Christmas Day,
Let's play and sing and shout hooray!

and the grown-ups turned their eyes towards the ceiling, and Auntie Bessie, who had already been frightened, twice, by a clockwork mouse, whimpered at the sideboard and had some

elderberry wine. And someone put a glass bowl full of nuts on
the littered table, and my uncle said, as he said once every year:
'I've got a shoe-nut here. Fetch me a shoe-horn to open it,
boy.'

And dinner was ended.

And I remember that on the afternoon of Christmas Day,
when the others sat around the fire and told each other that
this was nothing, no, nothing, to the great snowbound and
turkey-proud yule-log-crackling holly-berry-bedizined and
kissing-under-the-mistletoe Christmas when *they* were children,
I would go out, school-capped and gloved and mufflered, with
my bright new boots squeaking, into the white world on to the
seaward hill, to call on Jim and Dan and Jack and to walk with
them through the silent snowscape of our town.

We went padding through the streets, leaving huge deep
footprints in the snow, on the hidden pavements.

'I bet people'll think there's been hippoes.'

'What would you do if you saw a hippo coming down
Terrace Road?'

'I'd go like this, bang! I'd throw him over the railings and
roll him down the hill and then I'd tickle him under the ear
and he'd wag his tail ...'

'What would you do if you saw *two* hippoes...?'

Iron-flanked and bellowing he-hippoes clanked and blun-
dered and battered through the scudding snow towards us as
we passed by Mr Daniel's house.

'Let's post Mr Daniel a snowball through his letter-box.'

'Let's write things in the snow.'

'Let's write "Mr Daniel looks like a spaniel" all over his
lawn.'

'Look,' Jack said, 'I'm eating snow-pie.'

'What's it taste like?'

'Like snow-pie,' Jack said.

Or we walked on the white shore.

'Can the fishes see it's snowing?'

'They think it's the sky falling down.'

The silent one-clouded heavens drifted on to the sea.

'All the old dogs have gone.'

Dogs of a hundred mingled makes yapped in the summer at the sea-rim and yelped at the trespassing mountains of the waves.

'I bet St Bernards would like it now.'

And we were snowblind travellers lost on the north hills, and the great dewlapped dogs, with brandy-flasks round their necks, ambled and shambled up to us, baying 'Excelsior'.

We returned home through the desolate poor sea-facing streets where only a few children fumbled with bare red fingers in the thick wheel-rutted snow and cat-called after us, their voices fading away, as we trudged uphill, into the cries of the dock-birds and the hooters of ships out in the white and whirling bay.

Harri Webb
Christmas Cheer

Now every nation, land and clime,
Come join us in good cheer
And to our board at Christmas time
Bring what you hold most dear.

Before us mass the shining ranks
From north, south, west and east.
To one and all our hearty thanks
Who swell the season's feast.

First stand, in shapely bottles tall,
The vintage of the Rhine,
Bold hock, the noblest of them all,
Monarch of every wine.

Beside the king, behold the queen,
The nectar of Bordeaux,

Bright claret, still and cool and clean
As Pyrenean snow.

Around, like maids of honour stand
The rosé, red and white
From Austria's enchanted land
Of music and delight.

Chianti next, jester and wit
From sparkling Italy.
His wicker jacket's a tight fit
But his humour's broad and free.

In contrast see, aloof from sport,
From Portugal and Spain,
The proud grandees, sherry and port,
Look on in grave disdain.

And now we greet a cheerful lot,
And now we welcome in
From close at hand, Irish and Scot,
Our own convivial kin.

From stormy islands of the north,
From Islay, Mull and Skye,
From Spey and Tay and Clyde and Forth,
Whisky comes skirling by.

And Dublin city in her pride
Has conjured like a dream
The Liffey's black and magic tide,
Foam-crowned and soft as cream.

Gentle and simple, all well met,
Are gathered in one throng,
From Hereford and Somerset
Here's cider, yeoman-strong.

And, most familiar but not least
Of those who give us cheer,
The *gwerin*, backbone of the feast,
Our homely friend, good beer.

From every land beneath the sun
Here's spirits, wines and ales,
But above all lands there stands but one —
I drink the health of Wales.

Mike Jenkins
Turkeys Aren't Pets

Eat up your meat darling
especially the parson's nose.
No it's not from the nice vicar.
Yes, it's turkey dear
you know, gobble, gobble ...
of course, it won't make a noise.

Do you want breast? ... don't use that word!
I know it's got two of them.
Where are its feathers?
They were plucked ... I didn't swear.
Do be quiet, I'm only carving
because daddy's asleep in the chair.

Here, have the wishbone, pull it hard
it'll snap, wish for something ...
that doesn't look like its bum!
No, you can't keep turkeys as pets
(my god, he'll end up a vegetarian).

Robert Minhinnick
A Christmas Story

His neck stretched like one of his turkey hens,
Those most difficult birds to rear,
A wide crop exposed to receive the light.
And there he sways, a bundle of black feathers
Revolving on a chain in the sunlight,
An overcoat with the familiar gamey smell
And unpicked seam, but the face a stranger's,
Still snarling as when the muscles cracked.

Cold meat then: I can't say he's different.
Yet perhaps there's justice in this death.
Certainly his favourite story
Was a description of failure. His own.
A grown man with hands over his ears
Rolling on the floor of a darkened caravan
Like one of his own spent flagons,
As that bloody woman hammered, tore
Her hair and hammered to be let in
To a glow she had seen. But the door
Stayed shut as the caravan rocked back
On its axles, and a man lay in a pool
Of candlewax refusing to believe in
Another's despair, or the bundle of clothes
The express struck on the line.
But the verdict was in his eyes:
Murder, and indisputable guilt.
There is horror and it is here.

And it is here for one unforgettable
Instant as the news is broken over
Our dinnertable, over the bird that
Is itself broken between us,
Reduced to a shell of bone and crisped skin,
The dark meat and the white meat
Sliced away, and only its strange

Tube of eggs, like soft, yellow jewellery untouched.
For there are deaths and deaths and this one taints us.

Gwyn Thomas
Gifts

Christmas stockings were forbidden in the parts of the valley
given to mining subsidence. A heavily loaded sock would have
torn the bed apart. For three successive years I was given a
didactic annual called *Why and What*, but I kept so many
people on edge by going up to them and shooting at them the
questions that were answered in this volume I was lucky to get
through to Boxing Day unmaimed. 'Who was Colonel Fawcett?'
'Where is Caracas?' 'Why does the Mexican jumping bean
jump?' and so on. By family agreement the book was taken off
the list and replaced by one called *Cody, King of the Plains*, an
account of Buffalo Bill that slowed my mind down to a saunter.
I heard later that it had been a close race between Cody and a
book about missionary life called *Across the Great Salt Lakes
with Mary Slessor*. Cody won because my father couldn't stand salt.

Gifts of the fun, hedonistic sort were strictly out. If you asked
for a tricycle you were put out the back to cool. If you asked
for a pedal car you were given a rough little raft, shown the
Taff and ordered South. Or you might be beaten about the
head with a brass-bound edition of Benjamin Franklin's axioms
in favour of thrift.

Only once did I come anywhere near a lavish, frivolous gift.
I had an uncle who was a misanthropic shopkeeper. After a
stumbling attempt to get into undertaking, he had tried to start
a toy department but his face and temperament had damned
the project from the start. Not even a chain works could have
linked him with gaiety. His talking dolls snarled right back at
you and he was the one toy seller whose rocking horses would
have needed feeding. So he sold no toys and a pall of neglect
fell over that corner of his store.

One Christmas he decided to distribute every item of his old mouldering stock of toys among his younger relatives. My father told us to duck and he was right. To me came a vast box of lead soldiers. They were Welsh regiments in the varying uniforms of the last 200 years. The only garment they had in common was a heavy rust, for these pieces looked as if they had been minted over the same period of time as the uniforms. In my first attempt to set up a line of battle I impaled my finger on the bayonet of a crumbling South Wales Borderer and spent the first week of the New Year with a primely septic hand; it drove my father back to his traditional pacifism and gave my uncle his first sustained laugh of the decade.

Mike Jenkins
The Essence of Presents

Presents are all about revenge —
I send him Gerry Adams' latest volume,
he replies with an S.A.S tome.

They're to do with humiliation —
the time I got given
grandad's rusted tin-opener as an heirloom.

They're about total disregard —
my omnivorous son once sent
a boxful of dried vegan fare.

They're meant to baffle —
that plastic mosquito-net for cheese
we longed to use, but never quite ....

Presents are about forgetting ages —
as when my teenage daughter
received a second-hand Maths textbook.

And those telling phrases when giving —
like 'I've read it, it's really good.
In fact, it's the same one!'

Essentially they're about re-cycling —
that familiar wallet which does the rounds,
that bargain scarf I found.

Above all, they're about being grateful
that most of those kindly people
live too far away for a sly 'Thank you!'

Alun Llewelyn-Williams
Star of Bethlehem

This was a star that stood;
   but the law of the firmament is
when a star stands, it is dead;
   life is incessant force.

A witness to this rebirth,
   how is it the dead shines bright?
Poet and scientist search
   the whole creation's secret,

And the wonder of our wise men
   is the distant nebulae's speed
across the bounds of being
   and space to a fearsome void

from our insignificant world.
   And as their wheels whirl fast,
we see their old gleam coming
   from the inconceivable past,

like the buried sun's re-dawn,
    like a remembrance, that was, yet is from
the past that's eternally turning
    to a transient present, that will come.

But the whirligigs' hub always holds
    a sting of mortality,
so, when the stars disperse,
    dark and lonely our world will be,

and the scales in balance and empty
    and time annihilated.
But from the stillness the spirit
    that creates will once more be bred;

and this was a star that stood.
    From the boundless secret it came,
and the lustre of its tranquil look,
    that is not enslaved by time.

                translated by Joseph P. Clancy

Dylan Thomas
A Festive Letter to Pamela Hansford Johnson

                5 Cwmdonkin Drive,
                Uplands,
                Swansea.

                December 25th 1933

Another Afterthought: Christmas Day

    Thank you for the cigarettes. The Christmas dinner over, and the memories of it — so far at least — more in the mouth than in the belly, I have been sprawling in an armchair, (yes we possess one), smoking the first of your so very kind and unexpected presents. While the family is collected around the wireless, listening to the voice of His Majesty, let me write a note to you to tell you how glad I was to read your last letter and how horrified to think that you thought Robert Graves necessarily indicated the return of John Player[1] .... And my style this gray December evening (a reference to robins will appear now any moment) is as heavy as the brandied pudding now rising in revolt, deep in the chambers of my intestines, against too much four-and-sixpenny port and vegetables.

Child: Mother, how many pips in a tangerine?

Mother: Shut up, you little bastard.

My gifts are arrayed in front of me: a startlingly yellow tie and a peculiar pair of string gloves from my sister; a cigarette case from my brother-in-law; ten cigars from my father; 50 cigarettes from a young woman in Battersea; a knitted thing from the manageress of the hotel near my Little Theatre; the complete Blake from another uncle; Mrs Munroe's 1923-1933 Anthology from a friend who writes communism; two James Joyce pamphlets from myself; while outside hangs a neat, but tight, black hat from my mother, who has despaired for some time of the curves and angles of a decrepit trilby. That is all; and though your gift will vanish far more quickly than some of the others, it will last far longer in my memory than any of them .... Goodbye until tomorrow, when I hope that the heavy, academic idioms of this note will leave me lucid enough to write more and at more considerable length. The wireless is continually re-iterating the fact that Christmas is here, but Christmas, for me, is nearly over. How many more Christmases will these old eyes be blessed to see approach and vanish? Who knows: one far-off day I may gather my children (though a resolution denies it) around my spavined knee, tickle their chops, and tell them of the miracle of Christ and the devastating effect of too many nuts upon a young stomach.

1. He sent her poems by Robert Graves; she sent him Player's cigarettes.

John Wain
Christmas in Gwynedd

Christmas Day dawned amid white, freezing mist. As Roger walked along the lane towards Gareth's, the bottles dragged at his pockets. The sun was a low red disc and the mist went all the way up to the sky. Even the tops of the mountains were not wholly clear.

He opened the gate, went across the field, and knocked on the cottage door. It was eleven o'clock; he had timed his arrival with some care, so as to be early enough to help with the preparations but not so early as to intrude on a scene of comfortable late rising. Evidently it was right: Gareth, in his shirt sleeves but shaved and combed, opened the door at once.

'Merry Christmas,' he said gravely.

'That's come true already,' said Roger.

He entered. The old woman was sitting in her accustomed place. She wore the usual brown cardigan, but over it, across her broad fleshless shoulders, she had arranged a fine fringed shawl, decorated with intricate needlework. Perhaps the needle that made those thousands of patient stitches had been her own, half a century earlier; perhaps her eyes, in their days of keenness, had put in all those hours of close and loving observation.

'Nadolig Llawen,' she said.

Roger felt exhilarated. His sense of occasion was roused by her Welsh greeting and her embroidered shawl. Yes, this was to be a special day.

From now on, the three of them spoke in Welsh.

Sit down, Gareth commanded, drawing up a chair for Roger. The fire was hot and clear; it must have been lit at least two hours earlier.

But I want to help, Roger protested.

You can do that by keeping Mam company. Nobody's allowed in the kitchen. I'm cooking the feast and what I've got is a secret till I bring it in.

Roger, willingly allowing Gareth to be captain of his own ship, hung up his overcoat ready to sit down. But first (why not?) he took out the bottle of wine, an excellent hock that he had chosen very deliberately from the stock of the best wine merchant in the district.

Here's something to wash it down with. It needs to be cold so I'll stand it outside.

Gareth took the bottle for a moment in his great hand.

Wine, eh? he said.

I thought I'd like to bring something, said Roger simply.

I'm a beer man myself. But it does no harm to break out of your habits now and then. I've got a bottle or two of beer in, and to tell you the truth I've opened a couple already, in the kitchen, while I've been doing the vegetables. If I mix my drinks too much, you'll have to put me to bed.

Laughter forced its way from the echo-chamber of his chest.

All cooks drink, said Roger. The heat of the kitchen lets them sweat it out.

He opened the door and put the bottle outside in the misty morning. A solitary crow alighted, eyed the bottle, and flew disappointedly away.

Phil Carradice
Christmas Day at Pembroke

Finally, it snowed.

Blackened, Breughel figures
on the frozen Dutchman's lake.
Gaunt, skeleton fingered trees
stoop at the gibbering boys
who ride their arctic bicycles
across the crackling ice.

Silently, the snow-flung day
Whispers to its end.
As snow clouds and the night
merge, indefinable,
the lights of all the world
begin to flicker on and glow.

Rhydwen Williams
Christmas in the Valley

Life was hard enough in the Rhondda Fawr and Rhondda Fach throughout the 1920s, as the civilized world, and the uncivilized, came to know full well. Unemployment became the pattern of men's lives, and the despair of those years was plain for all to see in the listless eyes and colourless cheeks, and quite a few slashed throats up on the mountainside. And there was hardly a Christmas, despite the ringing bells and steaming puddings and the stockings tied to bedposts like the wares of Johnny Onions, come over to Llwyn-y-pia from Brittany, that didn't mock a small child's dreams and expectations.

For all that, I can't say that I ever failed to enjoy any of the Christmases in that far-distant childhood of mine, nor that I had to go without anything. Of course, neither my nose nor my senses had been trained to expect any special kind of luxury or delicacy, and I almost always had everything that was within the compass of my taste and desires.

The fact that I was brought up within a kitchen's snug wall was responsible, I'm sure, for the contentment I felt at the simplicity of the fare and fun. The word 'snugness' has a very special meaning for anyone who was familiar with the shelter provided by a collier's kitchen in days gone by — the special warmth from a coal-fire, a grate full of red-hot cheerfulness, when the dozing cats purred like a choir in four parts and the kettle whistled as merrily as a row of sailors just landed on a quayside.

On Christmas morning, like any other morning, one of the homeliest features of that long-ago snugness was the large frying-pan hissing fat as it prepared the bacon and eggs for us. The festive meat — whether pork, chicken, turkey or goose — could scarcely have tasted better between a child's teeth, and the bacon and eggs far excelled any slice of bread with honey on it.

But thinking of Christmas morning in times gone by brings back to me, more than anything else, the aromas of a busy, happy kitchen, with Mam getting us ready for chapel, my father in his white apron ('to save your suit'), and a spit hanging over a large fire, and the goose or turkey on it, a bunch of sausages dripping from the chains into the ashes, and a huge plate catching the fat. My father sweated before the flames even more than the bird. The wheel went round like a clock slowly turning, until the fatted goose was drier than the cork-stoppers of Mrs Evans Small Beer.

Whenever we look back like this and start talking about 'the old days', nothing is likely to be emphasized more than the poverty and hunger and misery of those years. And yet, when we go into more detail, the most lasting impression is of a festival of tremendous eating, when we stuffed all sorts of delicacies into our bellies — Welsh cakes, bread-pudding, apple-tarts and rhubarb-tarts, not to mention pea-soup, bacon baked with cheese, liver-and-onions, and the thick gravy tasting better than rice-pudding, almost. I feel sorry for those wretched people from North Wales who know nothing of these dishes but who are inveigled by the smiling courtesy of Hywel Gwynfryn to demonstrate their ignorance of things culinary on 'Helo Bobol' with recipes for meals that are a mess of grease and vegetables and hot curry, though they are acquainted only with takeaways from a Chinese restaurant. When I was a child in the Rhondda a Chinaman's only function in the community — with all due respect, for I have fond memories of old Harry Sing — was to iron shirts and collars. Now they starch our food as well.

The only bird that managed to escape its fate for a while was the one my parents refused to feather, let alone put to the knife or throttle, and that was because of the great commotion the Christmas before. We had a large goose, which we'd been keeping in the coal-shed for weeks, and the creature had begun waddling into our kitchen and making itself at home in front of the fire. We had all grown quite fond of it and been amused at some of its tricks, swearing by the sounds it made that it was answering us in Welsh, duck-Welsh, until by the day of its execution it had become like one of the family. When my father, after long argument, came to wring the dear little thing's neck, the bereavement and our sense of loss over-whelmed us, so much so that none of us was able to put a morsel of that gander's flesh into our mouths. That was the kind of palaver associated with our feasting in years gone by.

Like everything else in the life of the Valley, Christmas came to an end in the chapels. Most of the villagers would go to a service, the 'listeners' (a breed apart from the 'members'), as well as absentees of long standing, would find a seat at the back or up in the gallery. One old tipsy fellow always pursed his lips and breathed in through his nostrils as he squeezed past the saints on his way to his seat, lest his breath cause eyebrows to be raised and eyes to flash. All the laughter and fun of Christmas would be stifled under a load of solemnity, like my father beating the bonfire out with his spade. But the festival's aromas would go on wafting through our nostrils for a long while afterwards, as real as the smell of the leaves and branches at the top of our garden.

translated by Meic Stephens

Iorwerth Peate
The Craftsman's Carol

Mary sat in a bare stable
with Jesus on his straw bed;
so mothers of the world, in joy,
sing to the boy who sucked at breast.

Potter, support a spotless song
for one who gave life to all clay;
let your wheel sing praise to God
for one who turned all death to life.

Let the carpenter sing a chant of praise
as he shapes his boards upon his bench;
let chisel and gimlet sing to God
for one who turned all death to life.

And you the blacksmiths, join in song,
let the iron anvils and fire sing,
let the hammers sing praise to God
for one who turned all death to life.

And you the weaver, at your loom,
sing as you throw the shuttle free;
let blankets sing their praise to God
for one who turned all death to life.

And let the turner gaily sing
as he works at the sycamore with his gouge;
let chuck and treadle sing praise to God
for one who turned all death to life.

And with you I too shall sing
to the Jew once who loved me;
let all the craftsmen sing praise to God
for Jesus who turned all death to life.

translated by R. Gerallt Jones

Alun Lewis
A Letter from India
(to his wife Gweno)

Xmas Day 1943

This is supposed to reach you on Xmas Day: like the greetings I sent last year from South Africa: so I'm imagining myself coming up the hill and kicking the mud off my boots on the worn old hedgehog of a mat you've got at the foot of your steps and knocking at your door and hearing the delirious mixing of laughter. I want to enter merrily and take the kettle off the fire for your mother, and re-introduce myself to the two children: I'd rather come by the door and the daytime than sadly to your window at night, in a gust of rain or a rattle of wind and doubt.

But the main thing I'm saying is — here is another Xmas and here we are Alive; and whatever troubles the world still has, let's let them be for today and be lucky and thankful and sturdy with hope and fortitude.

I need the simple virtues most; the new fangled nervous virtues have been a bit much for me. I want quieter steadier ways. The little house and the certainty that I know could exist for us in time's lap some time. Let's let it, shall we? Let's not bother our little heads and hearts overmuch. Let's have our Xmas in ourselves each to each, and not unhappily. I'm so glad you've gone home. I've just had your letter when you were home for half-term and it chirruped at me with the honey and the pollen of the children and the warm circle of light that keeps them safe. They'll be big and self-conscious when I see them perhaps, but I can see them and love them now.

It's Xmas dusk and I'm trying hard to put everything aside and come to you. How hard it is, how hard. My heart has grown a crust so that I can't break but it leaves my body leaderless and it just dodders and bustles alternately and everyone else is an object encountered en route and circumvented. And such a Xmas! Oh sweet, I'm sorry I'm such a crust. I went to the morning service and that's the only time when I could 'be' at all. And suddenly as we sang 'Hark the

Herald Angels sing', my eyes began to sob and something tender that I've been hiding, hiding even from myself, woke for a minute and wept. Oh I wish it were always awake and I always alive. Not a dud entertainments officer rushing from swimming regatta to whist drive with a concert rehearsal in between. Booh. I think it's all punk and I'm angry at all I've wasted. You waste nearly everything from which you withhold your heart and my heart has withdrawn itself for weeks now from my dead here. I want no army Xmas again. I can't bear them and wish they didn't exist. Yet our boys have had a bouncing time. They had a huge dinner. Our cooks have been keeping a chicken farm for days: a great slaughter and plucking last night of the skinny things, and a lot of lorries dashing back and fore: boys sticking up 'Merry Xmas to the C.O.' with cotton wool on the dining hall walls: and little piles by each plate — cigar, sweets, orange, banana, bottle of beer or 'cordial' and ten cigarettes. Last night a whist drive and a midnight service, tonight the choir, tomorrow night my concert party and the night after eight ladies from Poona who want to dance for the troops!

I've been very quiet myself and kept away from the drinking and song-singing in the mess. Last night in bed I lay awake and listened to the carols being sung in the two canteens and a bell being rung from the hut where the catholics held midnight mass — and I, like Faust, asking to be released. You chide me for being downcast and bedraggled of soul. I'm sorry for being like that. But I must go the way my imperative leads me — and I feel that this long trial and strain on the spirit is likely to be decisive for me. I believe I'm being true to the realities in feeling this way: India is really a great purgatory and so is the war, and so is the future we are facing.

Idris Davies
The Christmas Tree

It shone, it sparkled, it was bright
With all the stars of Christmas night,
And every child that came to see
And wonder at that shining tree
Made it more radiant, for those eyes
Lent it the joy of Paradise.

T.H. Parry-Williams
A Christmas Carol

Close to a quarter of a century since then,
The Christmas morning my father crossed the glen.

A hell of a thing for Death on that holiday
To come by, like Father Christmas on his way,

And take him from us, and with a single stroke
Turn the Feast of Birth to a Feast of Death, as a joke.

We knew Death was all around; but there was no need
For the sneak to show his power, and suddenly

Leap from his carriage, like a monkey-on-a-stick,
Or a circus midget demonstrating a trick,

And this after we had learned all of our lives
My Lord Death was the well-bred model of how one behaves.

But possibly, nevertheless, in this matter I
Am making a mistake. Who is there can say why

The Lord of Terror himself came with his skull to play
A trick on us on the Son of Man's birthday?

Maybe His Grace, after all, intended no mockery,
But was investing his visit with public dignity.

I beg his pardon for doubting his meaning this way:
I saw him come from the glen with his summons a later day,

One Sunday morning to gather my mother to his breast. —
I've given in completely: I take back my words.

translated by Joseph P. Clancy

Jean Earle
Holy and Practical Matters

Gold, frankincense and myrrh
Brought, unexpected, to the carpenter's house.
How would Joseph guard them?
All the thieves would know.

And Mary, in her diptych or triptych,
Upright in her blue,
Under transcendent Light; all her signs and keys
And roses about her ....
Untouchable by him (for the time being).
Toiling to the well, washing and baking,
Joseph's earthly sons, all to come?

Surely, there would be meat,
Entertainment, for the Magi
Mesmerised so far. Perhaps a goat
Killed on that Christmas Day, innocent blood
Carmined with prophecy. Perhaps an aunt

Or a sister, cooking, while the village juggler
Tumbled his skills for dear life?

So, such a long time after, without trust
But with hope and a wistful faith, we keep
Our Christmas; bringing to the house
Comforting symbols, greenery and candles,
Presents and food ....

If it should snow
How lovely is the peaceful fall of white
On our dark heats — relief
Surprising the hard desert of the world.

R.S. Thomas
Hill Christmas

They came over the snow to the bread's
purer snow, fumbled it in their huge
hands, put their lips to it
like beasts, stared into the dark chalice
where the wine shone, felt it sharp
on their tongue, shivered as at a sin
remembered, and heard love cry
momentarily in their hearts' manger.

They rose and went back to their poor
holdings, naked in the bleak light
of December. Their horizon contracted
to the one small, stone-riddled field
with its tree, where the weather was nailing
the appalled body that had asked to be born.

Saunders Lewis
Carol

On the ancient tree sprung from Adam's grave,
Jesse's black and knotted trunk,
Was grafted a branch from heaven, and today,
Oh hosanna, Oh hosanna,
See — here is God's own rose.

In the starless night, no moonlight,
The pit of winter, in the year's
Senility — behold, a Baby,
The Son of Mary, Oh Sibyl,
The king of heaven was born.

Let a robin sing in the snow,
Let Melchior sing to his camels,
Let Vergil sing with Buddha:
Son of Mary, Alleluia,
Eia Jesu, Alleluia,
Praise to his name, all praise.

translated by Joseph P. Clancy

D.J. Williams
A Pagan Custom

... The woodcock is a difficult bird to get, they say, unless you
have the secret of its sudden turn in flight, but it is not nearly
as bad as the snipe. The best way to bring down a snipe is to
hit it straight after it has risen, before it begins its artful dodges.
In flight it looks like a sixpenny-piece wagging on a string in
the wind. And that used to be the price of the bird, too. Many
pounds have been spent in trying to hit down this sixpenny-
piece. And as this venturesome bird, the quicksilver of the
bogs, is not likely to cross our path again, I had better close

my account of him here by relating the incredible fact that I, yes, I, the poorest shot in the seven counties of the south, once, on my own, brought down a whole snipe to the ground. (The fact that it was a sheer accident is neither here not there. A fact is a fact.) And that was on Christmas Day in the morning, too. It was a custom of ours, and a pagan one it was, in the upper part of Llansewyl parish, the part which belonged to the Rhydcymerau district, to go out shooting on Christmas morning. In the afternoon and evenings the big annual eisteddfod was held. We went shooting for the fun of being out together, instead of in the women's way when they prepared the dinner, as no work was done that day. By that time of the year there wasn't much game left, only a bird or two that had been, as it were, purified through fire. But the birds of the dispersion would gather again, wonderfully, and a few along with them maybe from the edges of the adjoining estates, by mating- and nestmaking-time in the spring. If a hare started between the bushes of small gorse on the hillside or out of a clump of rushes on the bog, it was all the better for that. And if it escaped by the skin of its ears, as it were, after a few shots had whistled past it, well, that too was all to the good, as we might get a litter or two of her young by the following winter. However, the remnant of the birds must have been hiding very close that day, or, perhaps, like the domesticated ones, the geese, turkeys, fowls, and guinea-fowl in Idwal Jones's song, they had recollected that Christmas was coming in these uncivilized parts and had taken flight over the hills to a more Christian region, for the only thing that was started after a whole morning's walk was that fated snipe. And as there was nothing else to do with the cartridges I remember how at last I caught hold of the stocks of two guns, one in each hand, in the foolhardiness of youth, and, stretching my arms up, I fired off the two into the air at the same time, like a sort of Buffalo Bill handling his pistols. Incidentally, this was the last Christmas for me before leaving home for the first time, never to return to its full citizenship.

translated by Waldo Williams

Angharad Tomos
A Domestic Scene

When my father opened the door, I didn't know how pleased he was to see me.

'Now you're arriving,' he said disappointedly as I stepped through the doorway, saw his eyes, and stepped back to clean my shoes on the mat. 'She's been all by herself through the morning getting ready.'

'Sorry.'

I almost added that Mam wouldn't have been all by herself had her husband agreed to help her, but I didn't. Either because he and I had grown older and more sensible, or because I felt sorrier for him now, I don't know. A bit of both, probably.

'Merry Christmas, Mam!'

'And to you too Ennyd. Roll those balls of stuffing in breadcrumbs for me, will you?'

And I rolled balls of stuffing in breadcrumbs thinking what had that to do with the birth of a Saviour, mixed with thinking about my presents, and looking forward to Her's company, and guessing what Pill was doing on Christmas morning.

'Pass me the bread sauce, please.'

'More gravy, anyone?'

'No thanks.'

'Is it cooked alright?'

'Yes my dear — as good as ever.'

'I didn't have as good luck with the sprouts.'

Yes, it was a Christmas dinner similar enough to every other one, similar enough to Sunday dinner except for the thousands of small bowls that dotted the table with their different sauces, and the stuffing, of course. Since I didn't eat meat, I had a mixture full of nuts, which is what I had in my parents' house every time I ate there, summer or winter. Mam tended to take the fact that I didn't eat her turkey almost personally.

'Busy now, Ennyd?'

'No, it's Christmas.'

'No — the business in general, I mean.'

'There's no shortage of plates.'

They didn't have the least idea what I did. 'The daughter's in the pottery business,' they would say to people; it sounded better than saying she painted plates. The conversation grated on jerkily.

But before long, the yearly ritual would come to an end and I would give a sigh of relief — until my father remembered about the crackers. I haven't got anything against Victorian Christmas customs, only that they work best with a large crew of people in a party, and then only if they're blind drunk. At those times, wearing paper hats is fun and even the jokes raise a smile, but, please, avoid using them in a company of three, especially when two of them are teetotal. For a few years now I had suspected that that was the only reason why I would be invited to Christmas Dinner at my parents — to give them an excuse to pull crackers. Fair play to him, my father was quite a master at the game — he would make sure that he held tight to the brown strip and his cracker would bang every time.

He put the fragile hat on his head and read the paper: 'What do you get when you cross an elephant and a kangaroo?'

Yes, we know — large holes across Australia. We had that one last year. To save embarrassment, we spent two minutes guessing what the plastic shape was lurking in the remains of the paper. Those completely worthless things which stay next to the kettle for six months 'in case the grandchildren come round'. When the grandchildren did come round, they had much more interesting things to do than play with the remains of crackers. Finally, after feasting on After Dinner Mints, the dinner would be officially over.

Mam and I would wash the dishes after Christmas dinner while my father slept in his chair. Mam's conversation would be the same every time — feeling sorry that my sister and I had left the nest and what would become of us all, and why is the sky blue? and so on. I would mutter under my breath at times like these, concentrating completely on drying the cup handles thoroughly and making sure the forks shone. I knew very well that what was lurking behind the conversation was the eternal prickly question, 'when are YOU thinking of marrying?'

translated by Claire Collett

Bobi Jones
Sickness at Christmas

Sickness came over you yesterday like a shower of brine
And such a weakening! Grown-ups are so limp
That when they droop it's scarcely noticed, but with you
The stars lost their spit, the frisking of the kid
Turned to cold stone; and your sap was mangled out of you ....
But look, Christmas came: here you are
On a morning full of yeast again, a dewdrop in mid-desert,
With the sun flinging singing on the trees beneath the quaking
   of their hearts
And squeezing them — a fleet of shoots sailing along each
   branch
With the sun above their shadows turning them into white
   fishes
Beneath the stroke of his long magic wand. Christmas is in fact
   a feast-day;
That's just like God, into the shepherds' mid-winter He
   brought a bud;
At the lowest point of night He put a fire. He always gives
A birthday party in snow. Thanks be to Him for a sign.

translated by Joseph P. Clancy

E. Tegla Davies
Reflections on Mortality

It was Christmas morning, and everyone's heart rejoiced to
recall the babe born in Bethlehem; but it was not above the
manger that the Master of Pen y Bryn spent the day, but above
the bed of Mathew Thomas, watching him smiling as he lay
dying, and facing the Great Nobleman in his Palace. He still
had this mental conception of the place. He had heard many
things about that land, but it was the last idea that stuck in his

in his mind, just as the last look at a friend lingers in most people's minds. His thought had never dwelt on that place so much, in a short time, as it had done since the previous night. He had always had a nebulous sort of idea about it, somewhere in the remote corners of his soul. He, too, began to yearn for a glimpse of that territory, a glimpse from afar, before he had to face it himself — so that he could grow accustomed to the land. Sometimes he felt that he, the Master of Pen y Bryn, would be awarded greater honours there than a mere road-sweeper like Mathew Thomas. And yet, come to think of it, how little he knew about the place Mathew Thomas had gone to, on the threshold of which he had felt so much at ease. He had listened to sermons all his life, and he recited prayers publicly, but how little he had received from the gospel and from prayer! The gospel had lulled him into thinking that he was not as other men, and if he could get the saints to shout 'Amen' when he prayed, he was well pleased with his prayer. For the saints, for him, were those who listened to him praying.

Often he had heard the hymn:

'Byth ni threulia

Tynion dannau'r delyn aur.'

('The taut strings of the golden harp will never wear away.') He had felt, in some vague way, that the saints lived in a nebulous world of harp strings. But Mathew Thomas could not play the harp or anything else; and he had smiled as he lay dying. He had not realised before how vast the creation is, and how mysterious the ways of God. According to his profession of faith up to now, they had both been as clear as that two and two make four.

After seeing that smile, the Master of Pen y Bryn indulged in a long, cumbersome and tortuous contemplation for days. The soul's journey towards the light is a tortuous, indirect one. He tried to explain the smile, and the world Mathew Thomas had gone to, but he could not force himself to look that world in the face ....

translated by Nina Watkins

Ifor Thomas
Christmas Drink

In kilner jars, sloe gin
stood in our kitchen.
Pierced berries clumped
like path lab specimens,
preserved ectoplasm,
or diseased organs.
Clear liquid turned pink,
then days later the black
of coagulated blood.

He and I sat through
that Christmas holiday,
sipped sloe gin
with nothing to say.

I watched the colour of the fluid in
my father's colostomy bag
change from black to urine
as his rebored urethra healed
enough for him to begin
to piss again.

Alun Lewis
Christmas Holiday

Big-uddered piebald cattle low
The shivering chestnut stallion dozes
The fat wife sighs in her chair
Her lap is filled with paper roses
The poacher sleeps in the goose-girl's arms
Incurious after so much eating
All human beings are replete.

But the cock upon the dunghill feels
God's needle quiver in his brain
And thrice he crows: and at the sound
The sober and the tipsy men
Jump out of bed with one accord
And start the war again.

The fat wife comfortably sleeping
Sighs and licks her lips and smiles

But the goose-girl is weeping.

Mary Davies Parnell
A Rhondda Christmas

In those days a chicken dinner was a rarity unless you happened to breed them and had bought chicks early on in the war, so sausages, chops, liver or rissoles were frequently consumed for Christmas dinner. My parents had attempted breeding hens but they caused considerable problems — the proper nourishing grain for them was generally unavailable, they wouldn't lay, and they kept escaping over the wire fence, hiding in outside lavatories and pecking at neighbours' carefully grown vegetables. They caused chaos in the back gardens, because our own garden was too small for them to strut around freely and they destroyed the herbs, which were the only plants we ever grew. It was such trouble keeping them, we usually killed them after a few months and ate chicken dinners on consecutive Sundays in mid-year. They were skinny, scrawny birds anyway and not fit for a Christmas feast.

Every Christmas, Tydraw provided us with a well-fed, tender young chicken, bred in situ and far more successfully than our back garden fowl. For some reason the Tydraw bird was always presented to us live and we could choose which one we fancied for our dinner. First it needed catching and my father would resignedly undertake and finally make the capture after first having an undignified chase around Cae Bach, once causing the unfortunate bird to take refuge down the well and almost drown. Once seized, the squawking, indignant creature was bundled into a sack, which was quickly tied up. Whatever the weather it was necessary to walk back to Trehafod over the mountain as my father couldn't very well take a thrashing, protesting monster chicken in a sack slung over his shoulder onto the bus. Once home, it was allowed to roam in the cellar until evening, the eve of Christmas Eve.

Then, when all was quiet, when the sounds of socialisers returning from the Vaughan's Arms had faded and bedroom lights in neighbouring houses had been put out, my farmer's-daughter mother, well practised in the art, would quickly and neatly put paid to the chicken with a sharp knife by finding a special nerve in the roof of its mouth and, with a quick stab, puncturing its brain. The blood would be allowed to drip down the drain in the back yard. My feelings were in turmoil: pity for the chicken but admiration for my mother. Even if cast on a desert island, as long as she was there, we would survive.

'My father was the expert at this,' Mam would say. 'When he killed a chicken, you hardly had to pluck it. The feathers would fall off.'

Apart from the initial cacophany when taken from the cellar, it didn't utter a sound. Later the poor thing, with its limp neck hanging to one side, was brought into the kitchen for plucking, which was most easily done when the body was warm, and more easily still if the killing had been carried out properly and the special nerve found. Then methylated spirit was poured onto an enamel tart-plate, set alight and the naked chicken moved over the flame to burn off the hairs.

By the time the chicken had been stuffed and trussed, I had stopped feeling sorry for it and was eagerly looking forward to its succulent slices on my plate. I would pray for its soul in church in the morning.

John Idris Jones
Berwyn Christmas

The Tanat Valley drives like a broken arrow into the Welsh mass of the Berwyn mountains. It is joined by the river Rhaeadr just below Llanrhaeadr-ym-Mochnant. Above the village, a single-track road twists through Commins and Tyn-y-Wern until it faces that tall silver streak of water, Pistyll Rhaeadr. Here, on Boxing Day, I heard the cracking of guns, the brown blur, the brush tail and the never-before smell of the dead fox.

The Rhaeadr's water has flown through the air at the Pistyll, descended a thousand corners to the village, flowed under the bridge that marked the boundary between Denbighshire and Montgomeryshire and curved around the church under the steep tree-black slope of Pen-y-walk, polishing its stony floor all the way.

Just up from the village, set deep in woods, above the fresh water of the Rhaeadr, was, of all things, a canal. It was man-made, a neat trough, its waters sluggish, its light brown bottom of mud clearly visible on a bright day. It ended at the turbine house, inside which a huge metal wheel turned. When turning slowly it uttered a low groan but when the flow of water was good it turned with a happy hum. Along a path and over a stile was a field with cows. Inside its door one could see rows of dials and switches. This was the empire of Mr Smith the Electric. When the lights at home went dim and yellow we knew that the turbine was not able to do its work, too many leaves in the water perhaps, or not enough rain. Then domestic oil lamps would flame into life. But at night, seldom would the wallpaper be so entirely lit that one could discern the pattern through the room entirely. The picture-rail was stained brown and pictures hung from it from copper clasps. Brown flex hung along it at Christmas and twirled around the tree in the corner. Mr Smith would call and make these arrangements, a taciturn English man. A man who had moved large quantities of earth, who made the turbine spin, who had erected wooden poles along the margins of our streets, hung wires, yet there he was, with fairy-lights. I particularly liked the round ones, but the pointed ones had their charm too. I held the round one in my hand: it was a strange colour, like the egg of a rare bird, but corrugated. When lit, in the corner of our room, it gave off a yellow light; inadequate according to the science of voltage, but fitting. It was part of the gift and magic of Mr Smith.

In the dining-room the table was laid. It had a white cloth; cutlery came out of the wooden box under the sideboard. Silver holders were placed for the carving knife-and-fork. Their bone hands were grasped in my father's safe hands and before the carving there would be a sharpening of the knife on the stone. The kitchen had been in maximum use. Its grate and two green-flecked ovens well stoked-up, surrounded by steaming saucepans. Mother, in a navy-blue dress, came out of the kitchen carrying dishes and inside the dining-room took off her apron with deliberation. Father's bald head caught the light as he bent over the bird. Over our full plates we said a prayer in Welsh: *Diolch i Dduw am ein bwyd ac am ein ....* Under our bent heads we echoed *Amen* before raising the heavy cutlery.

The anticipation of Christmas is like no other; it is on the calendar once a year only. I was sent to bed early and traced the outlines of flowers on the wallpaper only briefly before sleep. Once there was an interruption, probably caused by the door opening. I saw in the gloom the figure of my father enter the room, carrying a pillowcase. He hung it over the base of the bed, its contents with their straight edges catching the moonlight. I knew that out there there were people who loved me — much better than Santa Claus — and I drifted back to a happy sleep.

When Nain and Taid came, there was a full house. They had been brought in our black Austin Twelve car, over the cob at Porthmadog, through Ysbyty Ifan and along the mountain road hanging above Llangynog. Nain used two sticks to walk and blocked up the corridor for ages as she shuffled from room to room. But my frustration at this ('Nain, fedra'i basio...') was tempered by her smile and bright eyes and musical voice. She had a Meirionnydd accent and used words foreign to me: 'da-da' for sweets and 'cyflath' for toffee. This was Grandfather's speciality. 'Mae Taid i yn neud cyflath' marked a special Christmas-eve activity. The heavy-base saucepan was found and he set to work, laying out the ingredients carefully. The brown liquid frothed and bubbled as he stirred with a wooden spoon, under his Roman nose and white hair. He melted butter before the fire and used it to grease two flat tins. He poured the lava-like substance into the middle, half-an-inch thick. After it had cooled a short time he drew regular lines in it with the end of a spoon. Then we had to wait. After testing it with his thumb, it was 'Mae'r cyflath yn barod' and he would crack it with a small metal hammer. He put the pieces in a tin with white powder and shook the tin. In the drawing-room, under the coloured lights, it was handed around. There was chewing and cheek-bulging and eyes showing approval. 'Ydi'r cyflath yn dda?' had to be answered 'Mae'r cyflath yn dda iawn, Taid.' That the toffee was excellent marked the quality of Christmas and the quality of family, where my grandparents stood for ritual and continuity.

When they sat around the Christmas table with their coloured hats on, Nain and Taid were like the King and Queen. She with her elaborate Victorian blouse with raised shoulders, fine hair, gold-rimmed spectacles, fingers bent with arthritis and bamboo sticks hooked over the back of the chair. Taid with his extraordinary resemblance to David Lloyd George, his hero; his hair down over his ears, dark suit with waistcoat, silk polka-dot bow tie. He was a deacon at Capel Garth. His near-flamboyance was matched by his gravitas. He made large-scale comments: he pronounced 'world' with a serious rolling of r's. He had a shelf-ful of books by and about Lloyd George. His conversation was punctuated by words from those politics: Asquith, Treaty, First World War, Munitions, Sylvester, Megan. Also constant in him were boxing, and *The News of the World*. He listened to the radio — a large bakelite box with fat buttons: his large ear would be bent to it hours at a time. He insisted on hearing boxing commentaries. As he picked up the sounds of fists flying his head jerked from side-to-side and his white hands jabbed the air. And on Sundays, between Chapel, he would lie on the couch in the drawing-room, away from us, and scan the pages of *The News of the World* with a studied un-lasciviousness.

His other daughter — Aunty May — lived in Spain. Each Christmas we would get a parcel of presents from them. There was usually a wallet and a tie. The wallet was soft and fine-stitched. The tie was silk, long, thick and in rich colours of blue, red and green. These items entered our utilitarian world like tokens from a place with much greater style and status, of sun, theatre, romance.

Around us, in Llanrhaeadr-ym-Mochnant, the shoulders of the hills pressed in upon our village. At Christmas it is as if the year holds its breath, and forgetting the tempo of everyday life — its regular Fridays and Mondays — slowly exhales, giving an unexpected day or two of quiet detachment. In 1946 we had it really: snow and snow and snow until the landscape above the sunken Llan was like the moon, white and flat with hedges buried and only the tops of telegraph poles visible. Outside my window, the snow filled the tiny street. It was awesome. Rooks cawed with fury, and the scraping of shovels against stone continued for weeks. You could hear the thump of snow-laden branches falling off the trees. But when the thaw and the Spring came, the swifts built their hanging pockets of mud as usual under the broad eaves of our home and the veils of ice that lay over the stones in the river melted and allowed the Rhaeadr to sing its way along. It still does.

Saunders Lewis
Under the Mistletoe

Christmas was drawing near. Every evening Bob MacEwan came to the house and he and Hannah put up holly and mistletoe and paper lanterns in an attempt to dispel its dreariness and gloom. Despite her father's misgivings, Hannah took on a girl to work in the shop over the festive season, added substantially to the usual stock of luxury goods, decorated the window, and turned her initiative into profit. Her father said:

'You're going to leave me just when you've got the business in hand. This is the first Christmas we've shown a profit.'

Mr Sheriff bought a bottle of port wine for Christmas lunch and Bob MacEwan was invited.

'I think,' said the father at table, 'that you and Bob shouldn't wait two years until you can afford a house. You ought to get married in the Spring and come here to live. You, Hannah, can go on helping in the shop and Monica can have a maid to help her. It'll be a fair deal.'

There was a toast to future success and the lovers' eyes sparkled as they raised their glasses. After lunch, Monica could no longer bear the glow on their faces. She went to her room that was on the same floor as the parlour.

'I'm going to lie down,' she said.

She took off her clothes and put on her dressing-gown of pink silk and swansdown. She stood before the mirror gazing at her reflection. The wine had brought out bright red flushes on the skin of her forehead and cheeks. She could see that her mouth was half-open and the tip of her tongue resting on her lip as if she were thirsty. But she did not try to compose her face, as she was wont to do. Instead, she listened. She heard the parlour door being opened and the couple laughing and whispering at the top of the stairs.

'Hurry up,' whispered Hannah, under the mistletoe, and Monica listened intently to the sound of kissing. She scarcely noticed that her own lips were pursed as she did so. Hannah ran up the next flight of stairs to her room, calling: 'Give me three minutes while I dress, wait there for me.' At this Monica picked up a towel and sponge as if she were on her way to the bathroom. She opened her door and went out onto the landing. Bob MacEwan caught her under the mistletoe and pulled her to him, kissing her. Suddenly he felt two lips prising his apart and a tongue licking under his own. Then, shocked, he let go of her and she slipped back into her room. Not a word had passed between them.

translated by Meic Stephens

Denis F. Ratcliffe
A Difficult Christmas

Christmas that year was more difficult than the previous year. Presents from 'Father Christmas' were smaller, chocolates and cakes were fewer, though the family still enjoyed a huge turkey on Christmas Day and for many days afterwards as usual. There was great fuss over mixing the Christmas pudding, and the ceremony of dropping in sixpence pieces wrapped in greaseproof paper was excitingly the same. This year the sixpences were replaced by silver threepenny pieces. D.'s sister Dot stole one of these, ineptly, before it was wrapped up and dropped in, and the loss was noticed immediately. There were only five of them anyway. D.'s father took over when his mother announced one missing. 'Right!' he declared officiously. 'We'll conduct a search. If it isn't found, the guilty one will be punished.'

This non-sequitur brought a ghost of a smile to his mother's lips.

The threepenny piece was not found. D. was questioned closely, since he now had a pedigree of theft dating from the plundered Christmas chocolate log, but nothing was proved. His mother glared with disbelief as he denied knowledge of the missing coin, but he escaped punishment, despite her muttered threats.

D.'s mother got into a bad mood on Christmas Eve, and it grew into a snappy bad temper by Christmas Day dinner. His father was silent most of the time and stayed in the parlour, reading. Christmas dinner was a trial, his father bossily and officiously carving up the turkey whilst his mother spent most of the meal ticking-off D. and his sisters about table manners. 'Don't hold your fork like that. Like this.' She would demonstrate while the culprit studiously looked away. 'Look at me when I'm talking to you,' she would snap. 'Like this.' The other two children would watch furtively, glad they had not come under attention, fearful of the next rule that would include them.

The meal was miserable, the children constantly nagged for

petty infringements of table manners, their father silent as he shovelled forkfuls of food in a way which seemed to D. none too polished anyway. He wondered if his mother would mention this until he saw that his mother took licence with her own plate. She shovelled away like his father.

The Christmas pudding went, accompanied by loud complaints from D.'s mother about the amount of time it took to prepare, and the few minutes it took for everyone to eat it. Next came the chores of clearing the table and washing up. Each of the children was designated a task, carried out under the merciless eye, and tongue, of their mother.

After the chores their father retired to bed to recover from the heavy meal. The children were commanded to play with their toys quietly. Overseen by their mother who sat in an armchair in the room, Dot had less opportunity to wreak her special brand of disruptive mischief on the other two, managing to engineer only two rebukes for them. Both parents found it easier to chastise the victims of her spitefulness rather than her herself, since she would, like Violet Elizabeth Bott, scream and scream at the smallest excuse. She had learned of her mother's fear of 'What the neighbours would think', and squeezed maximum advantage from it. She smiled with pleasure, and a sense of achievement, her eyes glittering with malice at her siblings' distress as they laboured under the injustice of a tongue lashing which she was fully aware was her own due. Snatching a toy not hers, breaking deliberately a vital piece, hiding another treasured item, claiming absurdly a possession clearly not her own, silently and with venom, all actions guaranteed to cause loud protest; these were her weapons to compensate for being the youngest, and number five in the pecking order in a family of five.

Margiad Evans
Christmases

When we were children
Christmases used to come in from the woods —
We fetched them, trundled them, sledged them, stole them,
The frost on our faces: the branches nodded their beards,
And the moon was gray on the bent, cold, grass —
Cat-ice crackled its broken glass
Like fireworks under our feet as we snapped it.
Christmases used to come in from the woods!
Gloria in excelsis Deo.

Tonight is Christmas again and I am sitting alone
Weave sleep for my child in my arms,
My arms which are forced
Into the old cradle shape, a bitter woman, ill to the bone.
There is never a Christmas night for me in this world again,
For I am not a child;
Christmases used to come in from the woods
Old and wild
But never alone
Gloria in excelsis Deo!

A.J. Cronin
Tom Evans' Pride

Next morning, Christmas Day, came fine and clear. Tallyn
Beacons in the blue distance were pearly, with a white icing of
snow. After a few morning consultations, with the pleasant
prospect of no surgery in the evening, Andrew went on his
round. He had a short list. Dinners were cooking in all the little
houses and his own was cooking at home. He did not tire of
the Christmas greetings he gave and received all along the
Rows. He could not help contrasting this present cheerfulness

with his bleak passage up those same streets only a year ago.

Perhaps it was this thought which made him draw up, with an odd hesitation in his eyes, outside No. 18 Cefan Row. Of all his patients, apart from Chenkin, whom he did not want, the only one who had not come back to him was Tom Evans. To-day when he was so unusually stirred, perhaps unduly exalted by a sense of the brotherhood of man, he had a sudden impulse to approach Evans and wish him a merry Christmas.

Knocking once, he opened the front door and walked through to the back kitchen. Here he paused, quite taken aback. The kitchen was very bare, almost empty, and in the grate there burned only a spark of fire. Seated before this on a broken-backed wooden chair, with his crooked arm bent out like a wing, was Tom Evans. The droop of his shoulders was dispirited, hopeless. On his knee sat his little girl, four years of age. They were gazing, both of them, in silent contemplation, at a branch of fir planted in an old bucket. Upon this diminutive Christmas tree which Evans had walked two miles over the mountains to procure, were three tiny tallow candles, as yet unlighted. And beneath it lay the family's Christmas treat — three small oranges.

Suddenly Evans turned and caught sight of Andrew. He started and a slow flush of shame and resentment spread over his face. Andrew sensed that it was agony for him to be found out of work, half his furniture pawned, crippled, by the doctor whose advice he had rejected. He had known, of course, that Evans was down on his luck but he had not suspected anything so pitiful as this. He felt upset and uncomfortable, he wanted to turn and go away. At that moment Mrs Evans came into the kitchen through the back door with a paper bag under her arm. She was so startled at the sight of Andrew that she dropped her paper bag which fell to the stone floor and burst open revealing two beef faggots, the cheapest meat that Aberalaw provided. The child, glancing at her mother's face, began suddenly to cry.

'What's like the matter, sir,' Mrs Evans ventured at last, her hand pressed against her side. 'He hasn't done anything?'

Andrew gritted his teeth together. He was so moved and

surprised by this scene he had stumbled upon, only one course would satisfy him.

'Mrs Evans!' He kept his eyes stiffly upon the floor. 'I know there was a bit of a misunderstanding between your Tom and me. But it's Christmas — and — oh! well I want,' he broke down lamely, 'I mean, I'd be awfully pleased if the three of you would come round and help us eat our Christmas dinner.'

'But, doctor —' she wavered.

'You be quiet, lass,' Evans interrupted her fiercely. 'We're not goin' out to no dinner. If faggots is all we *can* have it's all we *will* have. We don't want any bloody charity from nobody.'

'What are you talking about!' Andrew exclaimed in dismay. 'I'm asking you as a friend.'

'Ah! You're all the same!' Evans answered wretchedly. 'Once you get a man down all you can do is fling some grub in his face. Keep your bloody dinner. We don't want it.'

'Now, Tom —' Mrs Evans protested weakly.

Andrew turned towards her, distressed, yet still determined to carry out his intention.

'You persuade him, Mrs Evans. I'll be really upset now, if you don't come. Half past one. We'll expect you.'

Before any of them could say another word he swung round and left the house.

Christine made no comment when he blurted out what he had done. The Vaughans would probably have come to them to-day, but for the fact that they had gone to Switzerland for the ski-ing. And now he had asked an unemployed miner and his family! These were his thoughts as he stood with his back to the fire watching her lay the extra places.

Tom Macdonald
The Christmas Eisteddfod

Our Rosie was hired one November for seven pounds a year as a farm girl. She went to Blaenwaun, a farm beyond the old churchyard in Llanfihangel. In addition to the seven pounds she would be given a goose at Christmas, and when she went Christmas wasn't far away. She brought it home one Christmas Eve, already plucked and its flesh yellow and fat. It sat in a dish on our kitchen table and our mouths watered. It was the first goose I ever remember coming to our house.

On Christmas morning I watched our mother preparing it while Mary helped her to stuff it. I helped by stoking the fire while it cooked. It came out all shining and brown. Our knives were always blunt but the flesh of that goose came off so easily. There were lashings of it for everyone, for it was a giant goose. The taste of it. I doubted whether the Greek gods who dominated my reading then, had ever tasted a better meal. We licked our fingers.

'It's champeen,' said our Da. 'Best I've tasted since one of me uncles stole a goose one Christmas down Carmarthen way.'

'I thought your family was honest,' I challenged.

'I was a bit of boyeen then,' he said. 'I'd nothin' ter do with the stealin'.'

We praised our Rosie to the skies.

In bed that night Johnnie got to wondering how he could breed geese. He went to sleep before he could decide.

That Christmas time a girl down the road, Elizabeth Ann Spedding, who lived with her aunt Jane and Uncle Dai, who was a gardener at the Gogerddan mansion beyond Bow Street, said to me 'Why don't you come and recite at the eisteddfod in the chapel?'

She had learned the piece for reciting for the under-eights, she said, and it was called 'Y Llygad, y Trwyn a'r Sbectol' ('The Eye, the Nose and the Spectacles'). These talked to each other in the verses.

That night as we were hugging the fire I announced: 'I'm going to recite at the eisteddfod in the chapel at Christmas.'

'Why not?' said our mother before our Da had realised what I had said.

Then he said: 'No son of mine will ever enter that goddamn chapel.'

'Wot's wrong with it?' asked our mother.

'I want to win the shilling,' I said. 'I've never had a shilling.'

'Is that the first prize?' asked our Da.

'Yes,' I said.

'Yer think yer could win it, young 'un?'

'Maybe.'

'It don't mean that if yer recite in the chapel yer've got anythink ter do with their religion,' said our mother.

'None o' them prayers,' said Da.

'No,' said I, 'just singing and reciting.'

'And yer'll not let them Welsh childer beat yer?'

'I'll try hard to win.'

He gave in because, he said, I would be reciting for Ireland.

Elizabeth Ann went to Davies schoolmaster and asked him to teach her how to recite the piece. I went to Dewi. I had often seen him going off with his bag, which had his initials DM on it, when he went to judge elocution and poetry in the eisteddfodau in the other villages.

He beamed when I told him my mission. Only a few days before in the warm stable he had asked a cluster of us children what we were going to do when we grew up and I had said promptly: 'I'll write a book.'

'I wouldn't be surprised at that,' he had said.

Memorable nights by the kitchen fire at Garnhouse, I standing in the middle of the stone-flagged floor saying the piece, Dewi sitting on the settle. First time I rattled it off. He was hard to please.

'Speak with your face and your eyes,' he said. 'Watch your breathing. Bring the picture out. And your voice — it must carry.'

Sometimes his lovely, white-haired old mother listened to me, and one night she said: 'You'd think he was a little Welsh boy, Dewi.'

The suppers I had there. Plenty of butter on the bread. And boiled eggs.

'You got to be strong to be a reciter,' she said.

I whispered the piece by our own fireside, in bed, on the way to school. Some of the children mocked me. 'Think you've got a chance, Tommy tins, against us? You're not even Welsh.

You've never been on an eisteddfod stage — you'll be scared to hell.'

It became known that Johnny tins was sending his Tommy bach to recite against the Welsh children. God, the cheek!

On the night before Christmas Dewi didn't once pull me up as I went through the piece.

'Very good,' he said.

I knew then that I had reached the mountain top. As I was leaving his mother gave me threepence. It would cost that to go in to the eisteddfod.

At home they shone my boots, brushed my hair, scrubbed my face and nearly washed my ears off that Christmas evening before I went to Garn chapel.

I paid my threepence. I sat in a polished pew. The chapel was full of people. My palms sweated as I listened to a bunch of boys and girls, all under eight, reciting the piece. Little madams and misters, shining in their best clothes. Not one looked nervous. I was trembling when I went on the stage. My knees half buckled. The audience became a blur. I spoke with my eyes and my face. I made a few gestures. I heard the ring in my voice ... Finished. There was a tremendous crash of applause and I knew I had done well.

The judge was a stocky, long-haired man. He sat looking at his notes while the children under eight were at the singing competition. I thought they would never end, and when they did my heart hammered because the recitation judge was talking. On and on. He came to Cymro bach (the little Welshman) and that was me. His words burned into my mind and I would remember them all the days of my life.

Mary Davies Parnell
Sampling the Wine

As the morning wore on, the pans simmered or bubbled away, near or on the fire, each taking its turn to repose on the red coals or have its chance on the gas fire to speed the cooking process. Occasionally water boiled over onto the flames, which then made a dreadful fuss, hissing and spitting and steaming so that Peter would back away uncertainly from his place on the mat and seek a surer refuge under the table, his anxious brown eyes peeping out from time to time. Meanwhile the face of the cook was gradually going puce in the intense heat. The moment when the cooking of the bird was completed was fraught with anxiety. As the shop was open until mid-day for the people to collect their Christmas orders, a customer would come ostensibly to help manoeuvre it out of the oven but in reality to have a glass or three of elderberry, parsnip or rhubarb wine. In fact there was a constant stream of customers coming into the house on Christmas morning to sample the home-made wines, or at least what was left of them after several bottles had, as always, popped their corks with a loud explosion, not unfamiliar in those war days, and sprayed the wall-paper with delightful-smelling but distasteful-looking purple or yellow stains. My father started with communion wine early on Christmas Day and, steadily topping up with home-made during the morning, drinking the health of practically all his customers, he presented a beaming face and expansive disposition to his Christmas dinner, then spent the afternoon sleeping it off, the only day in the year when he took to his bed (apart from the annual 'paddy').

Tony Curtis
Christmas Poem at Tenby Harbour

The harbour huddles its few craft
Into the cold, calm pool of shelter
Beneath the white and yellow bright hotels,
As they return glassy stares to this Christmas Day.
Spray bites back at the sharp wind
As waves run their hag-grey kisses

Against the numbness of the harbour wall.
An old rum of a seagull bunches his neck,
Buff-feathered into his shuffling body
Muffled round with cold, as he picks
Along the curling line of water.
Four yards out from the brine wash
An abandoned summer speedboat is a scar,
Wood festered by the last gnawing of waves,
Rolling over, belly-swollen to the out-of-season sky.
The iced air cuts us clean apart,
Focussed in foreground to the scene as
Our chill, narrow gazes cover the dim
Horizon blend of featureless cloud and sea;
Survey the insistent rolling of the waves
Hands clasped firm together against all the new years.

Ray Milland
The Day of Delights

It was getting close to Christmas, that most wonderful and exciting time of gifts and expectation, a white and quiet world, where it seems to me the only sounds one heard were the voices of children. We would go bucketing down the hills after school in the moonlight in tin washtubs, homemade sleds, feed pans, anything that would slide. My favourite was an old Welsh coracle, a sort of fishing boat made to hold one man. It was constructed of long thin hazel wands woven like a basket and heavily tarred on the outside. Almost circular, they were used mostly on the great salmon rivers like the Usk, and the Severn and the Dee. In those days mine was not a polluted world but a world where gypsies camped and pheasants flew. And where children still believed in Santa Claus.

Above all, Christmas was the time of the Panto. Pantomime is a theatrical institution peculiar to Britain. The show is always based upon some legend or fairy story, like 'The Sleeping

Beauty' or 'Cinderella' or 'Jack and the Beanstalk,' which is transformed into a glittering musical extravaganza. There is always a Prince Charming and he is invariably played by a girl, while the parts of the older females are played by men. Most of England's great comedians and tragedians have also played 'dames' at some time or other. Indeed, they've looked forward to it with a great deal of relish. Three of the best in my memory were Sir George Robey, Sir Seymour Hicks, and George Jackley, all veterans and all stars ....

Yes, the 'dames' had a high old time on the stage, but I'm sure they would never be tolerated in any American family theatre today, even in this present age of permissiveness. Fifty per cent of the material would be blue-pencilled.

As Christmas Day grew closer, anticipation sharpened. By eight or nine o'clock we would be in bed, my sisters and I. But sleep was harder to come by; even with the bolster against the door I could hear them whispering and giggling, and then the carollers would come. I would quickly pop out of bed, rush to the window, and there they would be with a candle or two. Five or six young people singing 'Ar Hyd y Nos' or 'Good King Wenceslas' and singing it very well, too. For in Wales every child is taught music in some form or another from the first day he starts school ....

Christmas was so much more enchanting when I was a child. There were no bleary-eyed Santa Clauses on every street corner begging for some charity or another, ninety per cent of which you've never heard of, every one of them ringing those damn bells. No rabid used-car salesmen drumming up business in moth-eaten Santa suits, no TV and radio pitchmen yammering away at the Yuletide spirit. What happened to the Christmas spirit? I'll tell you, my friends, it went. And the world went with it. Long before Christmas comes you're sick of the sight and sound of it. Today children look upon Father Christmas as something old-fashioned and quaint. I remember once dressing up for my own children when they were six or seven years old, and I've never felt quite the same since. They accepted my performance very politely at the time, but they never *said* anything. Sadly, I came to realise that I had embarrassed them.

But we believed in Santa Claus with all our might, and when the day of the opening of the Christmas stocking finally came, we crept downstairs very slowly with our eyes as big as saucers, half hopeful, half afraid that maybe Santa hadn't reached our house after all. And then, at the bottom of the stairs, the whole magic scene burst upon us — the bulging stockings hanging from the fireplace and the toys spread beneath the tree. And I remember the oranges, oh! the oranges; they're Spanish and very fragrant and the whole house smells of them. And there were other smells, of fruitcake and port wine and cigars. All these grown-up glamorous things were brought out and passed around at Christmas. The rest of the year might be a dull bread-and-butter existence, but this, this was the day of delights.

Stuart Nolan
An Adult's Christmas in Wales

December 20th - January 3rd

quarter turkey.
quarter chicken.
1 lb beef.
quarter lb lamb.
half lb pork.
4 fish.
12 lb potatoes.
4 lb carrots.
4 lb sprouts.
3 tins peas.
half lb Yorkshire pudding.
3 loaves bread.
1 lb cheese (assorted).
2 pints custard.
half apple pie.
quarter trifle.

1 treacle pudding.
1 portion xmas pudding.
6 mince pies.
3 salads (assorted).
9 bars chocolate.
3 pkts biscuits.
8 vol-au-vents.
8 sausage rolls.
1 curry (unremembered).
11 tangerines.
half lb nuts (assorted).

56 pints lager.
14 pints bitter.
10 pints guinness.
4 pints snakebite.
8 measures whisky & ginger.
6 measures vodka & orange.
half bottle whisky.
half bottle brandy.
3 bottles red wine.
1 bottle white wine.
6 cans lager.
4 cans guinness.
1 glass sherry.
1 glass port.
1 glass tia maria (unremembered).
2 snowballs.

295 cigarettes.
5 cigars.

12 games pool (won 6, lost 5, 1 void).
4 games dominoes (won 1, lost 3).
1 game darts (abandoned).
1 game piggy in the middle with
full beer can (unremembered).
12 plays jukebox.
4 plays bandit (unsuccessful).

3 vomits.
1 blackout (duration 2 hrs).
1 successful adultery.
5 attempted adulteries.
3 fights (undefeated).

'Well! It's a time for the kids isn't it.'

Boxing Day to Epiphany

Chris Bendon
Slow
(*In Memory of William Mathias*)

Musick of Christemas
has died. Lone farmsteads star
the long barrow of a *cwm*.
Within the lit lantern of
a farmer's former home
intoxication, discovering snow,
made the woods outside baroque,
a white and gold cathedral
for the natural religion of
Le quatro stagioni.

Now there is strife between
harmony and invention:
the month, Janus-faced,
has frozen its flow,
releasing a few allusive memories
like the river's obsession
beneath holly's decorations of frosted ice.
Look into shallows of memory.
See straws of reeds set
in bases of glass, no sound
except the rustling breeze.
Then a shotgun's report.

One wild duck drops to the water,
too slow for death's drum, abrupt
as the black retriever which paddles after;
the marksman is the truest
lover of nature, having a shot at
what will feed his soul.

The Teifi is the present tense
in the year's blocked arteries.

A widower X-rays his wife's shrouded grave.
Her face is vague as the sun today.
Tomorrow, once again, will be yesterday
but her Welsh is diminishing,
her *dim Saesneg* translated as her body
through this high-tech age. He knows about
cremation but the thought makes
a dizziness blaze. He knows about
the paupers' little unmarked graves.
Here, cold as her stone, is a holiday home.
His old one should be heaven,
what with the global village glowing
on his colour screen, the fashions, accents,
the video outshining the dull Welsh dresser.

In a bell's slow eternal interval
the afterlife is lived, contingent as
that beech on the skyline, clean as paradise.

Like the silence after great music
the snow is blank over rise upon rise,
the hills are hoisted like laundered sheets,
death's seasonal slopes are like an offering
of the world to what shines still
on the verge of genius.

                    He has recalled her features.

History is that puzzling light
which shadows the relief of 'Bethel', 'Hebron',
      'Eglwys'
as if these hills were biblical and vertigo gripped the
      mind.
Each Christmas a quotation of another Christemas;
the unwrapped a surprise though inwardly known,
the Meccano the recorder or computer
the clumsy metaphors for the soul.

Emlyn Williams
A Boxing Day Treat

... we all went by train to Chester: the matinée of the pantomime at the Royalty, *Dick Whittington*. Dad had assured me
the Cat was six feet high. We were the first in the Early-Doors
queue for the gallery: no stools, but mufflers and sandwiches.
As at the Hip, we boys were to go on ahead and grab the first
seats; racing up the endless steps, I heard the blithe clang of
the first tallies through the cubby-hole, tumbling out for *us*.
We settled in the middle of the front row, on old newspapers
Mam had brought; for thirty seconds, as I bit the cold rail and
looked down into the glowing emptiness, we possessed a
theatre, licensed by the Lord Chamberlain to the Welsh Family
Williams. We even owned the great sign behind us, 'Beware
of Pickpockets'.

   This was more special than the Hip even: the steady clamour
as the gallery filled, the smell of dust and soap and gas-jets, the
taste of the apple and orange passed along by my mother ....
Then, beyond the murmur of the milling auditorium far below
— fairy-story children in the boxes, with rows of chocolates
before them — a weird miaowing which for a second I took to
be the Cat stretching himself; when I realized it was the
orchestra tuning up, I leant back, rapt, against a strange pair
of knobbly knees. The overture, my first, made the Hip piano
sound meagre indeed — 'Give me a Cosy little Corner', 'Let
the Great Big World Keep Turning', 'Goodbye-ee!' — and
then the curtain superbly rose — I remembered la Belle Russe
at the Opera House — on the glitter of colour, the sheen of
silk tights, the shrill babble of voices; the Williamses had been
swallowed up into the great family Gallery, a silent constella-
tion of eyes sharper than Dick's cat's eyes, all glittering watch-
fully in the dark. For me the magic of the Pictures was to stay
supreme, in a pantomime there was nothing for me to identify
myself with, but the Royalty had cast a spell which was still
over me as we drank tea in the pie-shop under the Rows before
catching the train. For several years the Boxing Day Matinée
was to be our treat.

Dannie Abse
Pantomime Diseases

When the fat Prince french-kissed Sleeping Beauty
her eyelids opened wide. She heard applause,
the photographer's shout, wedding-guest laughter.
Poor girl — she married the Prince out of duty
and suffered insomnia ever after.

The lies of Once-upon-a-Time appal.
Cinderella seeing white mice grow into horses
shrank to the wall — an event so ominous
she didn't go the the Armed Forces Ball
but phoned up Alcoholics Anonymous.

Snow White suffered from profound anaemia.
The genie warned, 'Aladdin, you'll go blind,'
when that little lad gleefully rubbed his lamp.
The Babes in the Wood died of pneumonia.
D. Whittington turned back because of cramp.

Shy, in the surgery, red Riding Hood undressed
— Dr Wolff, the fool, diagnosed Scarlet Fever.
That Jill who tumbled down has wrecked her back,
that Puss-in-Boots has gout and is depressed
and one bare bear gave Goldilocks a heart attack.

When the three Darling children thought they'd fly
to Never-Never Land — the usual trip —
their pin-point pupils betrayed addiction.
And not hooked by Captain Hook but by
that ponce, Peter Pan! All the rest is fiction.

Roland Mathias
After Christmas

Old berry and old sun
With other scantlings hang on
A bone from the lost tribe
Convivial song

Sloe like the slow minute
Wrinkles on stick: tooth in it
Bites through the fur to plum
Protestant virgin

Dark needle and dark pine
Bed down the trodden cone
A catholic fret for seed
Ground to the maiden

All humours and all wills
Consult the dark: except fools
Trading a whisper that the Child
Is back from Egypt.

James Williams
Killing the Pig

One of the most important tasks of the year was to slaughter
the fat pig, which weighed as a rule anything from sixteen to
twenty score live weight. It was not strictly speaking, a task,
more of a ritual, a blood sacrifice. The carefully selected pig
was well fed, from the time he was chosen for his high destiny
till the moment of truth on a cold winter morning, when he
was betrayed by those whom he thought were his friends. The
final stages of his diet consisted of milk, potatoes, and plenty
of barley meal. Any old crusts of bread, and scraps from the

145

table were added as tit-bits. Like the victim chosen for human sacrifices in ancient times, nothing was too good for him. No processed fish-food was ever fed to him, as the fishy taste would persist after death in the meat. The pig's bed was plenty of clean straw, changed regularly, into which he would burrow and relax into a nourishing 'fattening' sleep. The ceremonial slaughter of the sleek beast would take place around Christmas, or the New Year, and always during a waxing moon, never when it waned. I was always informed by the local wise men, that the bacon from a pig slaughtered when the moon was 'on her weakness' would not cure properly, and would be heir to most of the consequent blemishes, rancidity, mould, slime and even worse.

R.S. Thomas
Song at the Year's Turning

Shelley dreamed it. Now the dream decays.
The props crumble. The familiar ways
Are stale with tears trodden underfoot.
The heart's flower withers at the root.
Bury it, then, in history's sterile dust.
The slow years shall tame your tawny lust.

Love deceived him; what is there to say
The mind brought you by a better way
To this despair? Lost in the world's wood
You cannot staunch the bright menstrual blood.
The earth sickens; under naked boughs
The frost comes to barb your broken vows.

Is there blessing? Light's peculiar grace
In cold splendour robes this tortured place
For strange marriage. Voices in the wind
Weave a garland where a mortal sinned.
Winter rots you; who is there to blame?
The new grass shall purge you in its flame.

Dannie Abse
Something Ending

Looking out towards Somerset, I thought how I would dread being out there on a bucking ship in that fairground, switchback, elephant grey Bristol Channel. Not that one single boat was visible. Indeed, nobody appeared to inhabit the numb, land-locked afternoon either. Ogmore seemed nerveless, deserted. Some sheep huddled behind a stone-armoured wall, a few separate silhouettes of seagulls were flung off course, lifted giddily wide and high against the sky, and an idiot tin can, animated by the relentless wind, scraped the macadam as it bucketed past me, its sound diminishing with each step I took.

Though it was still afternoon, the lamp-posts began to glow. Soon it will be the shortest day of the year. Tomorrow we return to London. This will be our last sojourn in Ogmore this 1993. And, somehow, when I opened our wooden gate, I had that old familiar sense of something ending, 1993 going out as I was coming in. Perhaps it was something to do with the impending early darkness and the fury of the wind — something like a regretful au revoir, a smileless valediction, an end of a book also which, however, possesses a few blank pages after the print has run out. The coalhouse door was flapping and I bolted it tight. Inside the safe house the wind was defeated despite the rattling windows.

Francis Kilvert
Braving the Snow Storm

New Year's Day 1879

I sat up last night to watch the old year out and the new year in. The Church bells rang at intervals all last night and all to-day. At 6 I went to Crafta Webb to begin my cottage lectures there. It was raining fast when I started, but when I got as far the Common I noticed that the ground was white. At first I thought it was moonlight. Then I saw it was snow. At Crafta Webb the snowstorm was blinding and stifling, and I passed by Preece's cottage where I was going to hold the lecture without seeing it in the thickness of the driving snow. Before the lecture I went in to see old John Williams. On opening the door I was confronted by the motionless silent figure of a person veiled and wearing a conical cap which I presently discovered to be a dead pig hanging up by its snout. John Williams deplored my being out in such a night and said it was not fit for me. There were not many people at the service but the usual faithful few. When I came back the storm was worse and so thick and driving that I was glad I was between hedges and not out on the open hill. The young people at the servants' party seemed to be enjoying themselves with dancing and singing. After supper they came into the dining room to sing to me each with a comical cap out of a cracker on her head.

Siân James
Grief

My mother's prepared a beautiful dinner to celebrate the New Year: a roasting fowl with potatoes and sprouts and all the trimmings, followed by the Christmas pudding which Fredo, who'd tasted some the previous year in camp, had insisted should be kept for me. The table is beautiful: the lace table-cloth, made by my great-grandmother and shown in the Great Exhibition in 1851, two tall red candles in a pair of heavy brass candlesticks which are always on the table for any celebration but never lit, and the best dinner service, a wedding present, grey leaves on a white background, which comprises in all thirty-six plates, four meat plates, two tureens with covers and two gravy boats with ladles, which no one but my mother has ever been allowed to wash or dry.

'Is it still complete?' I ask my mother, 'this dinner set?'

Other families might boast a wireless set, an indoor lavatory or the electric light; we had a complete dinner service.

'No, not now, girl. I broke a plate on the day of your father's funeral and then poor old Davi Blaenhir broke another as he was putting it away for me.'

'Nothing lasts for ever.'

'Nothing lasts forever except longing.'

I sing the old song as she brings the dinner to the table:

> Derfydd aur a derfydd arian,
> Derfydd melfed, derfydd sidan,
> Derfydd pob dilledyn helaeth
> Ond er hyn, ni dderfydd hiraeth.

Nothing lasts except grief.

D. Parry-Jones
'Dydd Calan'

On the day itself we had, it is true, our turkey, but we did not make much of it; our big day was New Year's day. Feathering involving at least two days and two nights, was a communal activity of an extremely cheerful and boisterous character. As a large number of geese and turkeys were reared on the farms, at least a dozen helpers would be required and once the work had started, it went on day and night without a stop until it was finished. There was generally one woman who was the life and soul of the company; anyhow, peals of laughter would rise to the rafters as they gave themselves to work and to fun. Christmas day itself was spent quietly, the young men going out in small parties to shoot; visitors might perhaps turn up in the afternoon. There used to be a service in the parish church in the early morning at 5 a.m. or 6 a.m. called 'pylgen'. It was evidently a survival of the midnight mass. Pylgen still survives in many churches — and chapels — in those parts, where at one time it was the custom for each worshipper to take with him a candle.

Our big day was 'Dydd Calan' — New Year's Day. In this we resemble the Scots. After dining off goose, we went in the afternoon to the sports, organised by the local inn-keeper and his friends, and held in a neighbouring field.

There was some very fine running, especially, in the longer races. You will be able to imagine the physical fitness of these country lads when I say that they never smoked or drank, lived on plain, wholesome food, went to bed with the sun and spent all day in the open air. Why, they could run all day!

On this day large numbers of children went round the farms soliciting 'Calennig' (pennies). I do not remember that they had any doggerel to say or sing, but simply wished all a happy New Year — 'Blwyddyn Newydd dda'. It was not thought quite proper for the bigger farmers to send their children. Not only the children but women came too from the surrounding cottages and were given bread, cheese, milk and oatmeal.

Soon after midnight on New Year's morning, two or three companies of singers would come round the farms singing carols and other popular songs. These would be given a substantial silver piece and, if well-known to us, would be asked in to sing and partake of seasonable refreshments. Their stay would not be long as they had many places to call at, and it was their rule never to sing after daybreak. You will never hear them to-day, the 1914 war put an end to them, like many other things. It was an eerie experience to wake up on a dark, blowing, winter night to the echoing volume of manly voices underneath your window. Having rendered their songs and received their 'calennig' you could hear them tramping down the farm-yard and in a short time the barking of dogs at the next farm showed that they had turned up there.

Brenda Chamberlain
On Bardsey

Flocks of starlings swept into the fields, power-diving the island from the north, making a noise like hundreds of yards of calico being torn apart. Hail broke white; massive thunderclaps burst over the mountain. A lugubrious raven passed slowly, head into the wind, croaking DOOM ON ALL YOUR HOUSES! We were filled as it were for the first time with the horror of winter's darkest days and nights, and looked forward yearningly to January and the first full moon of the New Year. It was necessary to strain patience and fortitude to the utmost and say, 'Even the worst weather ends sometime'.

There was a spectacular storm: hail and thunder and darkness at noon, succeeded by blue sea and sky towards Ireland. The house windows reflected a sudden wash of light, the panes taking on the opacity of blind eyes. The solitude had a ghostly quality. Other people are necessary to us, if only to convince us of our own reality. As the bleak, storm-ridden days of darkness went slowly by, the spirit of life slowed until the women were reduced for gossip to what came to be known among us as 'Mouse-talk'; quite literally, we were debased to comparing notes on the mouse-life in our houses.

Christmas came and went; fires smoked sullenly. No greetings cards decorated the mantelshelves, but we made a crib in a corner of the study, and constructed a tree out of twigs from the tamarisk. We found a few sprigs of berried holly behind the chapel.

John Davies
The Comeback

'You the turn? Welcome to town,
squire. Interesting name: let's hope
the mike don't let you down.'

       Makeshift stage. M.C. humbly lowing
       in a barnlike room half-empty.
       Then, at eight sharp, the Coming.

'Can't dance! Can't sing!': in front
three blokes sprawled out like kings.
'Must be a joke, mate — a Rag Stunt!'

       Though the devil chills, warmth saves.
       Outside in the dark, gusts ride upon
       each other's backs in waves.

'Why didn't someone say? A sermon!
I'm off to check those bloody sheep —
then telly. 'Bye, all: must run.'

       The voice which, voyaging the room,
       has sailed serenely on towards the
       port of Silence, docks quite soon.

'Seen worse. No, it wasn't a bad draw,
not bad,' a wise man wisely said.
'Can't beat Max Boyce though.'

       All over? Here's to the girl who alone
       thought he really was the Greatest
       and told him so and walked him home.

Author's note: 'The Comeback' presents a club as if it were the stable at Bethlehem, with the three kings in attendance. The main act is Jesus in a Christmas comeback.

Tony Conran
Bethlehem

And wasn't I the Wise Man
At the end of it all?
        Mary, pray for him.
And didn't I bring him presents
        (Hear us,
        Elen of the way!)
Too little, too late for the half my life?

Gold I gave for his ending life —
And wasn't he the sick man,
        Mary of the way?
A battery shaver for his beard and all
        (Hear us,
        Elen, the way of him!)
Joy that I brought him presents.

Frankincense the next of my presents
And him rasping out his life —
        Mary, pray for him.
Signs I gave to a speechless man
        (Hear us,
        Elen of the way!)
Saying he knew what we meant and all.

But from Caer yr Aifft I carried all
My myrrh, my last of presents,
        Mary of the way!
Marged my daughter, my abounding life —
        (Hear us,
        Elen, the way of him!)
Wasn't he the proud dead man?

R.S. Thomas
Epiphany

Three kings? Not even one
any more. Royalty
has gone to ground, its journeyings
over. Who will now bring

gifts and to what place? In
the manger there are only the toys
and the tinsel. The child
has become a man. Far

off from his cross in the wrong
season he sits at table
with us with on his head
the fool's cap and our paper money.

Dannie Abse
Portrait of the Artist as a Middle-Aged Man
(3.30 a.m., January 1st)

Pure Xmas card below — street under snow,
under lamplight. My children curl asleep,
my wife also moans from depths too deep
with all her shutters closed and half her life.
And I? I, sober now, come down the stairs
to eat an apple, to taste the snow in it,
to switch the light on at the maudlin time.

Habitual living room, where the apple-flesh
turns brown after the bite, oh half my life
has gone to pot. And now, too tired for sleep,
I count up the Xmas cards childishly,
assessing, *Jesus,* how many friends I've got!

154

Author's Acknowledgements

My especial thanks to the following who wrote material for the book: Ifor Thomas, Mike Jenkins, John Idris Jones, Gladys Mary Coles and Jean Earle. I am indebted to Mick Felton who commissioned this anthology, and provided the overall critical perspective which was so essential.

I also wish to extend warm thanks to John Davies, Meic Stephens, Tony Brown, Jeffrey Robinson, Moria Dearnley and Sally Baker, all of whom, at one point or another during my research, provided the necessary stimulus which all anthologists need.

And the final words of thanks have to go my wife, Pamela, who kept me topped up with coffee in the small hours while I read book after book after book....

Publisher's Acknowledgements

Acknowledgements are due to the following for permission to reprint work in this anthology.

Dannie Abse: 'Pantomime Diseases' from *Miscellany One* (Poetry Wales Press, 1981), 'Portait of the Artist as a Middle-Aged Man' from *Funland and Other Poems* (Hutchinson, 1973); excerpt from *Intermittent Journals* (Seren, 1994) © Dannie Abse and by permission of Peters, Dunlop & Fraser Ltd. **Chris Bendon**: 'Slow' from *A Dyfed Quartet* (Headland, 1992) © Chris Bendon. **Ruth Bidgood**: 'First Snow' from *The Print of Miracle* (1978); 'Solistice' from *Kindred* (Poetry Wales Press, 1986); 'Magpies at Christmas' unpublished, all © Ruth Bidgood. **Richard Burton**: excerpt from *A Christmas Story* (Hodder & Stoughton, 1989) © 1965 the estate of Richard Burton. **Phil Carradice**: 'Christmas Day at Pembroke' unpublished, © Phil Carradice. **Gillian Clarke**: both poems unpublished, © Gillian Clarke. **Brenda Chamberlain**: excerpt from *Tide-race* (Seren, 1996) © estate of Brenda Chamberlain. **Bruce Chatwin**: excerpt from *On the Black Hill* (Cape, 1982) © 1982 The Estate of Bruce Chatwin, reprinted with the permission of Aitken & Stone Ltd. **Joseph Clancy**: 'A Cywydd for Christmas' from *The Significance of Flesh* (Gomer, 1984) © Joseph Clancy, by permission of Gomer. **Gladys Mary Coles**: 'Touching Balloons, Llandudno', unpublished © Gladys Mary Coles. **Tony Conran**: 'Bethlehem' from *Castles* (Gomer, 1993) © Tony Conran, by permission of Gomer. **Edith Courtney**: excerpt from *A Mouse Ran Up My Nightie* (Gomer, 1975) by permission of Gomer © Edith Courtney. **A.J. Cronin**: excerpts from *The Citadel* (Gollancz, 1937) © the estate of A.J. Cronin. **Tony Curtis**: 'Christmas Day at Tenby Harbour' from *Album* (Christopher Davies, 1974), 'The Infants' Christmas Concert' from *Letting Go* (Poetry Wales Press, 1983) © Tony Curtis. **E. Tegla Davies**: excerpt from *The Master of Pen y Bryn*, translated by Nina Watkins and published by Christopher Davies, 1975, by permission of the publisher. **John Davies**: 'The Comeback' from *At the Edge of Town* (Gomer, 1981) © John Davies, by permission of Gomer. **Idris Davies**: 'The Star in the East', 'The Christmas Tree' and 'Christmas Eve, 1946' from *Collected Poems* (University of Wales Press, 1995) © the estate of Idris Davies. **Janet Dubé**: 'Advent Poem for Jo' from *In Praise of Carnivores* (Gomer, 1997)

© Janet Dubé. **Jean Earle:** 'Holy and Practical Matters' unpublished, © Jean Earle. **Margiad Evans:** 'Christmases' first published in *Cornhill Magazine* © Cassandra Davis. **Peter Finch** 'Some Christmas Haiku' and 'More Christmas Haiku' © Peter Finch. Versions of some of these haiku appear on Peter Finch's web site. **Catherine Fisher:** 'Nativity' from *The Unexplored Ocean* (Seren, 1995) © Catherine Fisher. **Paul Henry:** 'Inside the MIND shop' first published in *Planet* © Paul Henry. **Richard Hughes:** excerpt from 'Strange Christmases' first published in *Harper's Bazaar*, December 1930 © the estate of Richard Hughes, by permission of David Higham Associates. **Siân James:** excerpt entitled 'Mother Christmas' from 'Maid in Heaven' published in *Not Singing Exactly* (Honno, 1996); other excerpt from *Love and War* (Piatkus, 1995) © Siân James. **Mike Jenkins:** both poems unpublished © Mike Jenkins. **Bobi Jones:** 'Sickness at Christmas' translated by Joseph Clancy and published in *Bobi Jones: Selected Poems* (Christopher Davies, 1987), by permission of the translator. **Glyn Jones:** extract from 'Rhysie at Aunt Kezia's' published in *Welsh Heirs* (Gomer, 1977) © Mrs D. Jones. **Huw Jones:** 'Christmas card' unpublished, © Huw Jones. **John Idris Jones:** 'Berwyn Christmas' unpublished, © John Idris Jones. **Alun Lewis:** 'Christmas Holiday' from *Collected Poems* (Seren, 1994); excerpt from *Letters to my Wife* (Seren, 1989) © the estate of Alun Lewis. **Eiluned Lewis:** excerpt entitled 'A Sad Dark Tune' (Penguin, 1947) from *Dew on the Grass*, other excerpt from *The Captain's Wife* (Macmillan, 1944) © the estate of Eiluned Lewis. **Saunders Lewis:** 'Carol' translated by Joseph Clancy and published in *Selected Poems* (University of Wales Press, 1993) by permission of the publisher and the Estate of Saunders Lewis. Excerpt from *Monica* translated by Meic Stephens and by permission of the translator and the Estate of Saunders Lewis. **Alun Llewelyn-Williams:** 'Star of Bethlehem' translated by Joseph Clancy and published in *Twentieth Century Welsh Poems* (Gomer, 1982), by permission of Gomer. **Hilary Llewellyn-Williams:** 'Holly' from *The Tree Calendar* (Poetry Wales Press, 1987) © Hilary Llewellyn-Williams. **Michael Gareth Llewelyn:** excerpt from *Sand in the Glass* (John Murray, 1943) by permission of John Murray (Publishers) Ltd. **Ronnie Knox Mawer:** excerpt from *Land of my Father* (Bridge Books, 1994) © Ronnie Knox Mawer. **Tom Macdonald:** excerpt from *The White Lanes of Summer* (Macmillan, 1975) © estate of Tom Macdonald. **Roland Mathias:** 'After Christmas' from *Snipe's Castle* (Gomer, 1979) © Roland Mathias. **Ray Milland:** excerpt from *Wide-Eyed in Babylon* (Bodley Head, 1974). **Robert Minhinnick:** 'A Christmas Story' from *Life Sentences* (Poetry Wales Press, 1983) © Robert Minhinnick. **Stuart Nolan:** 'An Adult's Christmas in Wales' first published in *New Welsh Review* © Stuart Nolan. **Leslie Norris:** excerpt entitled 'Great, Invisible Birds' from 'A Flight of Geese'. Other excerpt from 'The Wind, the Cold Wind' both published in *Collected Stories* (Seren, 1996) © Leslie Norris. **Mary Davies Parnell:** both excerpts from *Block Salt and Candles*

(Seren, 1991) © Mary Davies Parnell. **D. Parry-Jones**: excerpt from *Welsh Country Upbringing* (Batsford, 1948) © estate of D. Parry-Jones. **T.H. Parry-Williams**: 'A Christmas Carol' translated by Joseph Clancy and first published in *Poetry Wales*, by permission of the translator. **Iorwerth Peate**: 'The Craftsman's Carol' translated by R. Gerallt Jones and published in *Poetry of Wales: 1930-1970* (Gomer, 1974), by permission of Gomer. **Douglas Phillips**: 'Christmas at Pentrepoeth School, Carmarthen' first published in *New Welsh Review* © Douglas Phillips. **Denis Ratcliffe**: excerpt from *Second Chances* (Seren, 1996) © Denis Ratcliffe. **Dewi Roberts**: 'The Invitation' first published as 'The Kiss' in *Cambrensis* © Dewi Roberts. **Kate Roberts**: excerpt entitled 'Pricking the Bubble' from *Tea in the Heather* (John Jones, 1997) translated by and copyright Wyn Griffith, by permission of the publisher. Other excerpts from 'The Battle of Christmas' translated by Joseph Clancy and published in *The World of Kate Roberts* (Temple University Press, 1991), by permission of the translator. **Selyf Roberts**: excerpt from an essay translated by Meic Stephens and published in *Illuminations* (Welsh Academic Press, 1998) by permission of the translator. **Meic Stephens**: 'Dymuniad y Tymor' from *Exiles All* (Triskele Press, 1973) © Meic Stephens. **Dylan Thomas**: excerpt of letter from *The Collected Letters of Dylan Thomas* (Dent, 1985). Other excerpt from *Quite Early One Morning* (Dent, 1954). Both © the estate of Dylan Thomas and by permission of David Higham Associates and New Directions Publishing Corporation. **Gwyn Thomas**: excerpt entitled 'Ogley the Abstainer' from 'Bacchus Bach' published in *Ring Delirium 123* (Gollancz, 1960); all other excerpts from the essay 'Father's Christmas' © the estate of Gwyn Thomas, by permission of Felix de Wolfe. **Ifor Thomas**: 'Christmas Drink' unpublished, © Ifor Thomas. **Irene Thomas**: 'Christmas Goose' first published in *Poetry Wales*, © Irene Thomas. **R.S. Thomas**: 'Christmas', 'Hill Christmas', 'Song at the Year's Turning' and 'Epiphany' from *Collected Poems* (Dent, 1993) © R.S. Thomas, by permission of The Orion Publishing Group. 'Carol' from *Later Poems* (Macmillan, 1983), © R.S. Thomas, by permission of Macmillan. Excerpt from 'The Qualities of Christmas' from *Selected Prose* (Seren, 1995) © R.S. Thomas. **Angharad Tomos**: excerpt from *Wele'n Gwawrio* (1997), published by Y Lolfa cyf, Talybont, Ceredigion, Cymru, SY24 5AP, phone 0044 (0)1970 832 304 © Angharad Tomos. Translation © Claire Collett. **John Wain**: excerpt from *A Winter in the Hills* (Macmillan, 1970) by permission of Curtis Brown Group. **Vernon Watkins**: excerpt from 'The Ballad of the Mari Lwyd' from *Collected Poems* (Golgonooza Press) © Mrs G. Watkins. **Harri Webb**: 'Christmas Cheer' from *Collected Poems* (Gomer, 1995) © Meic Stephens. **Nigel Wells**: 'Y Plygaint' from *The Winter Festivals* (Bloodaxe, 1980) © Nigel Wells. **D.J. Williams**: excerpt from *The Old Farmhouse*, translated by Waldo Williams (Harrap, 1961). **Emlyn Williams**: both excerpts from *George* (Hamish Hamilton, 1961) © the estate of Emlyn Williams.

Herbert Williams: 'Billy Scrooge and the Santagram' first published in *The Western Mail* © Herbert Williams. **James Williams**: excerpt from *Give Me Yesterday* (Gomer, 1971) by permission of Gomer. **Rhydwen Williams**: excerpt from 'Christmas in the Valley' translated by Meic Stephens and published in *Illuminations* (Welsh Academic Press, 1998) by permission of the translator.

Every effort has been made to contact copyright holders, but if any have been overlooked the publisher will be pleased to make the necessary arrangements.

The following out of copyright material has also been used. **Thomas Love Peacock**: extract from *Headlong Hall* (1816). **Rowland Watkyns**: poem from *Flamma Sine Fumo: or Poems Without Fictions* (1662). Extracts by **Francis Kilvert** from his diary.

About the Editor

Dewi Roberts, who lives in Denbighshire, is well known in Wales as an anthologist. His regional compliations include *Vistors' Delight* and *A Clwyd Anthology*, and the next title in this genre, due out in Spring 1998, will focus on the Welsh Border Region. He has published a travel book, *The Land of Old Renown*, and is an essayist and reviewer for a number of publications. Apart from literature his main interest is local history.